Your Teenage Years are Over (or Almost) Now What?

Life Skills for Young Adults

How to Manage Yourself, Your Finances, and Your Relationships

NADIRA DAWN

BOOKS ARE LIFE
PUBLISHING

Your Teenage Years Are Over (or Almost) Now What. Life Skills for Young Adults. How to Manage Yourself, Your Finances, and Your Relationships.

Published by: Books Are Life Publishing

ISBN:9798218391577

Disclaimer Page

The information presented in this book "Teenage Years are Over, Now What? Life Skills for Young Adults" is intended to provide helpful and informative guidance on important life skills for teens and young adults. All materials, including text, graphics, logos, names, titles, etc. are provided for general information purposes only. The author and publisher make no representations or warranties concerning any information shared in this book and disclaim all liability for the use or interpretation of any information contained in the book.

The content and advice shared here are not intended as substitutes for professional services such as counseling, therapy, medical treatment, financial advising, etc. Nothing in this book should be construed as professional advice tailored to a reader's specific circumstances. If expert assistance is required, the services of competent professionals should be sought.

The author and publisher will not accept responsibility for any liabilities arising directly or indirectly from the information shared in this book.

Readers will assume full responsibility for the use to which they put such information. The sharing of stories in this book does not constitute an endorsement. All names and identifying details have been altered to protect privacy. Ultimately readers must use prudent judgment in applying any recommendations to their own lives.

Contents

Introduction

You likely feel both eager and apprehensive as you stand between adolescence and adulthood. You crave independence and responsibility yet need ongoing guidance and support in facing this new frontier.

The prospect of becoming wholly self-sufficient and contributing meaningfully to society can seem daunting without the proper life skills. This is precisely why I wrote this book – to equip you with the essential knowledge and tools to tackle adulthood confidently.

Within these pages, you'll discover a comprehensive guide to cultivating core competencies required to thrive at this stage of life. I've honed these lessons over 15 years of mentoring youth like yourself through their transition into "the real world." Time and again, I've seen newly minted graduates stumble when they lack abilities for independent living or practical know-how. Most desire to chart their course but feel unsure where to begin.

That's where this book comes in. By focusing step-by-step on building skills like self-discovery, critical thinking, time management, and money management, you can turn this period of change into a springboard for success. My anecdotes and advice come directly from the knowledge of guiding hundreds of teens like you.

My goal is to help young people know the fears and challenges you'll inevitably face are normal, while empowering you to meet them as a ready adult. Consider me your wise sister, here to remind you that you can not only survive but truly thrive in adulthood. The skills you develop now will serve you for the rest of your life.

So, let's embark on this journey together! With each page, you'll gain knowledge to conquer new milestones. When you finish this book, you'll feel capable of stepping boldly forward as the fully realized young adult you were meant to become. Turn the page, and let's get started building your launchpad.

Part I:

Managing Yourself in the Adult World

Chapter 1

Transitioning from Teenage Years: The Emotional Roller Coaster

I. Introduction

The transition from adolescence into adulthood can feel like an emotional rollercoaster. As a teenager navigating this turbulent period, you will experience rapid changes biologically, socially, and psychologically. While exciting, it is also overwhelming and unsettling at times. Learning to manage these changes smoothly is key to a successful launch into adulthood.

Physical Transitions

Remember when puberty hit you and all of a sudden, several changes occurred including rapid physical development marked by growth spurts and body parts doing things they didn't do before. The flood of hormones that activated puberty will continue to impact many older teens and young adults into your 20s.

The rapid physical growth of adolescence can trigger self-consciousness. Both males and females may feel uncomfortable and awkward in their changing bodies. Accepting and appreciating your mature body is essential for your self-confidence.

And guess what? With increased sexual maturity, you're about to dive into the world of desire and attraction. Balancing those natural urges with social norms, values, and safety is the name of the game.

In a nutshell, these physical changes have pushed you to redefine your self-image and your way of interacting with the world. Trust me, with some supportive guidance, this can be an exciting process of blossoming into young adulthood.

Cognitive and Social Transitions

You will also notice that your mental processes and reasoning abilities also mature along with your changing body. Your brain has been exhibiting increased neural connectivity and newfound cognitive skills around planning ahead, self-regulation, and abstract thinking.

With stronger logic and imagination, you start questioning the status quo and gain the capacity for moral reasoning. Psychologists Piaget and Kohlberg associated this "formal operational" stage with philosophical ideation, existential questioning, and idealism/cynicism cycles.

While this may be intellectually stimulating for you, the back-and-forth between imaginative hopefulness and harsh skepticism will often create emotional ambiguity and confusion. You will need to learn to balance wide-eyed dreams with pragmatic realism and this could be a tough but necessary part of your transition.

On the social front, you've likely started to shift away from your parents being your main influence. It's now all about those peer relationships—friendships, cliques, relationships, and cultural trends. Acceptance, status, gossip, and heartbreak, anyone?

Navigating these social waters is no joke. You're building strong bonds, but there'll be ups and downs. Social hierarchies can be volatile, and gaining communication skills is crucial. Your core identity? It's shifting from family-defined to self-defined and getting ready to figure out your autonomous self—you might feel a bit in flux, but that's part of the journey.

Psycho-Emotional Transitions

On the inside, you face a turbulent clash between your emerging adult self and residual childlike dependencies. Resenting external control while craving support, protection, and reassurance from authority figures like parents and teachers. It's a classic teen dilemma.

This internal tug-of-war might lead to moody outbursts, unpredictable behavior, and emotions all over the place. As you juggle grown-up privileges and responsibilities, anxiety and guilt might tag along. Your evolving values might clash with your childhood self, causing identity crises.

The solution? You will have to learn emotional regulation, distress tolerance and how to cultivate self-awareness around your complex feelings. Make yourself an active student of life by learning how to communicate your needs effectively and watch those bumps in the road smooth out. Developing autonomy while staying connected to support systems? That's your secret weapon against confusion, insecurity, and existential angst.

II. Understanding Yourself

"Know thyself" - this ancient Greek aphorism is perhaps more relevant than ever during the transition into adulthood. When you understand your core identity, interests, values, strengths, and weaknesses, you can live authentically and intentionally. Self-awareness is the foundation for emotional intelligence, fulfilling relationships, and pursuing well-suited opportunities.

Without knowing their true selves, young adults can drift aimlessly or allow others to define them. They construct their identity and direction in life largely based on the expectations of parents, peers, social norms or media influences. But these external sources often clash with their inner truth.

Getting clarity on who you really are beneath any labels allows you to shape your own identity and path forward. As you transcend the simmering insecurity of adolescence, self-understanding provides a steadying force.

The philosopher Aristotle called the deepest human drive "eudaimonia" - the desire to live out one's full potential. To achieve this self-actualization, you must first understand your distinctive gifts, passions, and purpose. Like a flower, you can only bloom when properly nurtured in the right soil under optimal conditions.

Without this personal insight, it is natural to experience angst and lack of fulfillment. You may continually compare yourself to others and always feel like you do not measure up. Or you may unconsciously mold yourself to gain love or approval while sacrificing what makes you unique.

In adulthood, defining yourself based on childhood programming or others' expectations is no longer sufficient. The buck stops with you. Therefore, the self-discovery journey is non-negotiable for anyone seeking to spread their wings fully.

As you quietly contemplate your inner landscape during this transitional period, certain truths will rise to the surface organically. Parts of you once suppressed due to fear or shame, may finally break free. Give space for your authentic voice to emerge before pursuing any major life decisions regarding relationships, education, or career.

While exhilarating, peering honestly into the depths within can also feel intimidating. Some conclusions may force hard choices or the loss of connections that once defined you. However, accepting even the painful or scary pieces is necessary to move forward from a place of wholeness. The most important relationship now is the one you build with yourself.

This self-discovery process requires brutal honesty, courage, and compassion. Be gentle yet bold in your commitment to shedding anything that obscures your inner light. You may not appreciate all that you uncover, but simply acknowledging the truth will empower you.

Here are key lessons to take with you on the lifelong path of self-discovery upon which you now embark:

Lesson 1: It Takes Courage

- Self-understanding requires radical honesty which can be uncomfortable at times. Admitting aspects of yourself that feel unpleasant or messy takes courage.

Lesson 2: It's a Continuous Process

- As you evolve, your sense of self will deepen. Revisit your truths periodically to integrate new insights. Self-discovery is lifelong.

Lesson 3: Go Beyond Surface Level

- Peel away the labels, masks and ego identity to connect with your core values, passions, wounds and motivations. Go deep.

Lesson 4: Observation is Key

- Tune inward through introspection practices to understand behaviors, thoughts, feelings. Self-awareness arises from observation.

Lesson 5: You Are Not Your Thoughts

- Don't attach your identity too tightly to stories or judgments in your head. Instead find the awareness behind your thinking self.

Lesson 6: Excavate Your Past

- Uncover how your upbringing and past experiences shaped you. Then decide what still serves you and what to release.

Lesson 7: Adopt a Beginner's Mind

- Inquiry into your whole self with an open and non-judgmental attitude. Pretend you know nothing about who you are and rediscover yourself.

Lesson 8: Make Friends with ALL of You

- Accept every aspect of yourself - beautiful and ugly, luminous and dark - with compassion not shame. Wholeness arises from integrating all your fragmented parts.

Lesson 9: Let Your Truth Guide You

- Once you know who you are beneath societal conditioning, let that authentic self direct your choices with courage.

Lesson 10: Comparison blocks Self-Knowledge

- When we focus on others, we lose connection with our inner truth. Cease measuring yourself by any metrics outside your own soul.

You alone hold the keys to understanding your distinctive brilliance and charting the optimal course for your life. Therefore, make the solo journey within among your top priorities during this transitional period.

So, in this transitional season, treat yourself to elegant stillness and regular silence. In the space between your thoughts, the light of self-knowledge awaits. With discipline, courage, and curiosity, embark on this lifelong adventure of self-discovery. It is your birthright.

How to Explore Your Identity, Interests, Values, and Beliefs.

Navigating the passage into adulthood feels more seamless when you have a clear sense of direction based on self-knowledge. An inner compass pointing toward your unique identity, passions, values, and beliefs keeps you oriented during transitional uncertainty.

Lacking this personal foundation, it is easy to feel adrift and defined by the expectations of others. You may continually seek external validation rather than trusting your worth. Without understanding your core self, important life decisions become overwhelming.

Therefore, consciously exploring the realm within is vital preparation for the journey ahead. Self-discovery is not self-centered navel-gazing, but rather bolstering your ability to live purposefully. Know thyself, and you need not fear forging your own path.

Here are strategies to illuminate understanding of your identity, interests, values, and beliefs:

Exploring Your Identity

Identity encompasses how you see and define yourself based on personality traits, roles, abilities, experiences, culture, and relationships. While parts of your identity may feel fixed, like your gender or ethnicity, other aspects are more fluid, like interests and tastes.

Start by taking inventory of all the labels used to describe you - are they accurate? Do any chafe? What roles do you play in various settings? How did your family shape you? What social groups do you identify with? Which feel inauthentic? Peel away any false masks to uncover your core self.

Spend time alone, without distractions, to notice your natural temperament and tendencies when you are not performing for others. Tune into your thoughts, feelings, and behaviors - are you inherently introverted or extroverted? Optimistic or cynical? Passionate or reserved? Sensitive or thick-skinned?

Journal freely to gain insight into recurring themes and patterns. What are your default defense mechanisms under stress? What charges you up and drains you? How do you typically relate to others? What stimulates you intellectually?

Review memories from childhood through adolescence and consider ways you have evolved. Appreciate all the experiences that have shaped you. But don't let your past wholly define you either - decide what still fits and what you have outgrown.

Identity journeys are lifelong, so enjoy getting to know yourself deeply over time through this process of mindful self-reflection.

Exploring Your Interests

Interests motivate you and enrich your life. They reflect talents, provide outlets for self-expression, and lead to communities of kindred spirits.

To identify interests, note what types of activities energize you. When do you lose track of time because you are engrossed in an activity? What topics could you chat about effortlessly for hours?

Scan your social media and browser history for clues about your interests. What online rabbit holes do you frequently go down? What magazines or books do you consume voraciously? Which websites, forums, or fandoms do you keep visiting?

Look back on peak experiences that stirred your spirit, like travels, festivals, classes, or conversations. Revisiting these high points provides hints about environments where you naturally thrive. Keep an ongoing list of your pastimes so you remember to integrate them into your routine.

Trying new hobbies or skills can also reveal latent interests. Step outside your comfort zone. Dabble in wide-ranging activities from sports to arts to volunteering. Pay attention to what leaves you feeling energized versus drained.

Make time for regular solo reflection, free-writing, or artistic expression. Your true interests may surface when you quiet outer noise and listen within.

Exploring Your Values

Values represent your core principles and ideals about life. They shape priorities, goals, behavior, ethics, and relationships. Understanding your values allows you to align your decisions with what matters most to you instead of what pleases others.

To identify your values, ask yourself open-ended questions: What is most meaningful to me? How do I want to spend my limited time on Earth? What principles guide my life? What is success to me? How do I want others to experience me? How would I raise my children? What matters at the end of life?

Look at people you admire - what values do they embody that resonate with you? Think of times when you felt most fulfilled - do any common values emerge? Consider moments when you felt distress or anger - are there values underlying those emotions?

Name values after self-reflection, then rank them by importance. Choose your top 5 core values. Is your current lifestyle honoring those values? If not, what needs to shift? Consciously orienting choices around your values yields alignment.

Exploring Your Beliefs

Beliefs are ideas you accept as true that shape how you interpret situations and interact with the world. Questioning beliefs you inherited from family, society or religion allows adopting perspectives closely aligned with your inner wisdom.

To identify beliefs, observe your spontaneous thoughts and stories about reality. What core assumptions fuel your instinctive reactions? Does everyone share those same ideas? Were you taught certain worldviews rather than concluding them yourself?

Examine each belief by asking - is this true or just a subjective opinion? Does this belief empower or limit me? Where did I learn this belief? Is it still serving me, or should I challenge it?

Instead of automatically accepting mental shortcuts like stereotypes, dig deeper. For example, reexamine any beliefs assuming human nature is fundamentally selfish or that your worth depends on productivity.

Practice mental flexibility by considering alternate vantage points. Hold opinions lightly without clinging to them rigidly. Stay open to updating your beliefs based on new life experiences that reveal deeper truths.

Exploring what lies within prepares you to encounter adulthood from a place of authenticity and personal authority. Know thyself.

Activities or Exercises for Self-discovery.

Embarking on the adventure of self-discovery during this transitional period will enrich your life journey. Here are engaging exercises to reveal your authentic identity, interests, values, and beliefs:

1. Childhood Time Capsule

Gather mementos from your childhood - old photos, report cards, drawings, birthday cards, trophies, etc. Review each item slowly. What clues do they contain about your innate personality, talents, interests, and relationships? Reflect on how certain traits have remained constant while others evolved.

2. Core Values Assessment

Make a list of words that reflect values like freedom, integrity, compassion, adventurousness, loyalty.

Review definitions if needed. Highlight ~10 values that most resonate with your spirit. Then narrow down to your top 5 core values. Keep this list handy as a compass for decision-making.

3. What Matters Most Before I Die?

Imagine you are 90 years old, nearing the end of your life. Write a letter to your present self about what matters most based on life lessons learned. What wisdom would your elder self share? What goals or dreams would they encourage you to pursue? What regrets would they warn you to avoid?

4. If I Couldn't Fail...

Make a list starting with: "If I knew I could not fail, I would..." Let your imagination flow freely without self-judgment. What activities, projects, and dreams would you dare pursue without limits? Your soul's purpose often reveals itself when you remove the fear of failure.

5. Past Peak Experiences

Make a timeline of your life. Note peak moments that stirred your spirit, connected you to life's purpose, or brought deep fulfillment - travels, books, friendships, classes, conversations, solitude in nature, etc. Do you notice any themes in these high points? What values, interests, and environments do they reflect?

6. Personality Test

Take a validated personality test like Myers-Briggs, Enneagram, DISC, or Big Five. Journal about your type description - what resonates and what doesn't? Consider growth opportunities based on your tendencies. Appreciate strengths and accept limitations with self-compassion.

7. Twenty Things I Love

List 20 things, people, places, activities, etc. that bring you joy and contentment. Include small pleasures like your morning coffee routine or chatting with your sibling. This reveals the moments when you are most authentically yourself. Find ways to integrate more of these into your regular life.

8. Advice to My Younger Self

Write a letter offering advice and reassurance to yourself as a child or adolescent. What guidance would you give your younger self based on what you know now? What core truths would you convey to help them feel understood and supported during the inevitable challenges of growing up?

9. If I Were 100% Honest with Myself...

Finish the sentence stem honestly, writing continuously for 5-10 minutes without self-censoring. What truths surface when you drop the pretense and judgment? Bring radical self-acceptance to any uncomfortable revelations.

10. 30-Day Gratitude Challenge

Start a daily gratitude journal. Write 3-5 things you feel grateful for each day for one month. Include people, experiences, senses (smells, foods), moments (sunset), and privileges (education). Did any themes emerge throughout the month that provide clues to what matters most to you?

By regularly engaging in these mindful self-discovery practices, you will gradually uncover your inner wisdom. Don't judge your insights - just observe gently and keep growing your self-knowledge. You may feel both drawn to and humbled by meeting your authentic self during this transition into adulthood. But with courage, creativity, and compassion, you will come home to who you were always meant to be. Enjoy the journey!

III. Managing Personal Changes

Strategies for Managing these Changes Effectively.

Ultimately, you inhabit an entirely new biological vehicle including altered brain functioning. The physical transformation can feel fun and exciting, but also uncomfortable and alarming. Strategies like the following help you adjust:

- Research the science behind these changes to normalize them.

- Discuss changes openly without shame or secrecy.

- If female, understand your menstrual cycle and track its effects.

- Practice body positivity and appreciate your uniqueness.

- Reframe growth spurts as signs your body is becoming stronger.

- Monitor energy and stay hydrated during rapid growth phases.

- Be patient with acne and treat skin gently without attacking blemishes.

- Find non-toxic remedies like exercise or meditation to balance hormones.

- Listen carefully to bodily cues and treat new aches right away.

- Maintain physical upkeep through nutrition, exercise, hygiene, sleep.

While physical changes largely unfold involuntarily, you always have agency over nurturing your body with great care during this sensitive transition.

Emotionally, moods fluctuate wildly, especially in response to physical and social triggers. Newly awakened sexual feelings stir up confusion and vulnerability. Teens feel the urge to individuate from parents, but still depend on their support, which creates conflict. Identity crises emerge as youth try on different personas and ideologies, which can spiral into anxiety or depression.

Managing these turbulent emotional changes calls for:

- Normalizing mood swings as growing pains, not personal flaws.

- Journaling, art, music, dance as healthy outlets for feelings.

- Building a toolkit of coping strategies like deep breathing, timeouts, gratitude.

- Talking through struggles without judgment from a trusted confidant.

- Not making big decisions impulsively based on temporary emotions.

- Considering long-term impact of your actions before reacting.

- Forgiving yourself when emotional flooding leads to regrettable behavior.

- Developing self-awareness around your unique emotional patterns.

- Knowing it's okay to rely on your support system amidst overwhelm.

Consider counseling if emotions become unmanageable. There is no shame in getting help learning to navigate new feelings.

Ultimately, you must balance integrating within your peer group while still honoring your uniqueness and values. Avoid compromising your core identity just to fit in socially:

- Cherish old friends while welcoming new social connections.

- Say no to situations misaligned with your values, even if peers pressure you.

- Recognize toxic friendships and tactfully distance yourself when needed.

- Join groups aligned with your authentic interests and passions.

- Appreciate companions who support your growth into independence.

- Date those who treat you like a valued partner, not just a social status symbol.

- Spend time with peers who share your goals and bring out your best self.

- Keep communicating with parents, even if you need space from them.

By proactively managing the multifaceted changes unfolding in all realms of your life - physical, mental, emotional, social - you can approach this transition with grace. Despite feeling like everything is changing overnight, you remain in control over nurturing your overall well-being. Your core spirit remains steadfast, even as your body and life stage transform.

Tips for Maintaining Physical Health during These Changes.

The biological changes and transitions that occur during the teenage years can be taxing on the body. Maintaining good physical health provides energy, improves mood, and enables better handling of emotional and mental changes. Here are some tips:

- Get enough sleep - Aim for 8-10 hours per night for optimal rest, growth and health. Practice good sleep habits like avoiding late night screen time.

- Eat a balanced diet - Fuel your growing body with plenty of vegetables, fruits, whole grains, protein and healthy fats. Avoid excess sugar and junk food which can lead to crashes.

- Stay hydrated - Drink enough water throughout the day, about 8 cups or 2 liters. Dehydration exacerbates fatigue.

- Exercise regularly - Get at least 60 minutes a day of heart-pumping activity to relieve stress and boost endorphins. Team sports provide social benefits too.

- Limit alcohol and drugs - These substances interfere with healthy development, compounding emotional volatility common in adolescence. Prioritize wellness.

- Get regular checkups - See your doctor once a year for preventative care. Monitoring growth trajectory spot treats emerging issues.

- Practice self-care - Listen to your body's needs and respond to avoid depletion. Healthy habits mitigate growing pains.

Remember that the discomforts of adolescence will pass. Support your changing body with nourishment, activity, and tender loving care. If you have specific worries, confide openly with a trusted grownup. Invest now in your well-being to thrive through the upcoming phases of life.

IV. Expressing Your Needs

Importance of Expressing Your Needs and Seeking Help

Transitioning into adulthood comes with heightened responsibilities. But expecting total self-sufficiency overnight is unrealistic. You will still need support, advice, and reassurance at times from those who care about you. There is courage in acknowledging you cannot - and should not - do everything alone. Learn to humbly express your needs and ask for assistance when challenges arise.

Why It Matters

Admitting vulnerability or lack of knowledge does not make you weak. Strategically seeking and accepting help demonstrates wisdom, self-awareness, and strength. We all depend on others for guidance along our journey. Allowing trusted allies to support your growth is far healthier than struggling silently.

Techniques for Effective Communication

Communication techniques like assertive speech, active listening, and "I" statements foster mutual understanding. They help you articulate your experiences while inviting others to do the same. Studies show open communication increases intimacy in relationships (Laurenceau et al., 1998). Simply verbalizing fears or confusion often provides relief.

Suggestions on who to approach when you need help – friends, family members or professionals.

Whom to Approach

Turn first to those who know you best and have earned your trust, like close friends or relatives. They offer insider insights about your unique personality and background. Tapping existing support systems is most comfortable initially.

But also expand your net, as different confidants can lend diverse perspectives. Older mentors who have walked in your shoes provide wisdom. Counselors have special training on adolescent challenges. Leave no potential stone unturned.

How to Ask

First, reflect inward on your underlying needs and feelings. Then, choose an appropriate setting to initiate a caring dialogue. State your request clearly and respectfully. Provide context to show you have reflected thoroughly. Express willingness to discuss solutions collaboratively.

For example, you might say, "Mom, I feel anxious about managing my schedule next semester. College seems so much less structured than high school. Could we brainstorm ways I can stay organized?"

Listen actively to their responses, ask clarifying questions, and express appreciation for their support. Remember, voicing needs is not about placing blame or pressure, it is tapping resources available to you. With courage, honesty, and gratitude, you will find the assistance required to spread your wings - even when the wind feels rough.

V. Navigating Unsettled Emotions

Adolescence brings intense cognitive, social, and physical changes. Your emotions may feel like a rollercoaster as you navigate this transition. Mood swings, anxiety, sadness, and irritability are common temporary reactions during this turbulent developmental period. Implementing healthy coping strategies can smooth out the ride.

It is perfectly normal to experience "growing pains" like:

- Anxiety about increased responsibilities or identity changes

- Low self-esteem from comparing yourself to peers

- Sadness over friendships/relationships ending

- Distress from family conflict as you individuate

- Frustration about lack of control over your evolving body

- Irritability from hormonal fluctuations

- Confusion over sexuality when puberty begins

While difficult, these emotions generally pass with time as you adjust. However, seek help if they persist at highly disruptive levels.

Coping Strategies Based on Cognitive Behavioral Therapy Techniques

Cognitive behavioral techniques (CBT) help manage challenging emotions. CBT focuses on replacing negative thought patterns with balanced thinking (Beck, 2011). Helpful CBT-based strategies include:

- Writing down irrational thoughts; then logically challenging their validity

- Channeling anger or sadness into creative outlets like art or music

- Making uplifting self-statements like "This too shall pass"

- Avoiding dramatizing situations as catastrophic failures

- Listing your strengths to combat negative self-talk

- Practicing calming rituals like deep breathing when overwhelmed

- Exercising to release pent-up tension or anxiety

- Calling a friend when lonely instead of isolating

- Scheduling pleasant experiences to boost your mood

Seek Professional Help if Needed

If difficult emotions persist despite coping attempts, consult a mental health professional. Therapists and counselors are experts at helping youth navigate adolescence. Ask your doctor for referrals. School counselors can connect you with resources too.

Consider joining a support group. Sharing your experiences with peers going through similar struggles reduces isolation. Virtual communities exist via social media.

Remember, you do not need to tough this out alone. We all need assistance sometimes. There is courage in acknowledging you cannot - and should not - do everything solo. Reach out and allow others to support you through this challenging yet beautiful transition.

VI. Conclusion

Integrating Your Experiences

Like a caterpillar morphing in the cocoon, you are undergoing a profound metamorphosis. As you transition from adolescent dependencies into adulthood freedoms, the process can feel mystifying at times.

By now, you have gleaned key lessons to equip you for this passage:

First, accept the emotional flux during this period as normal growing pains. Mood swings, insecurity, irritation, and sadness come with the territory. Be patient with yourself when you do not feel grounded. This too shall pass.

Next, embrace self-discovery practices to understand your evolving identity and needs during this transition. Explore your personality, values, interests, and beliefs. Check in regularly through reflection and honest dialogues with trusted allies.

Further, patiently nurture your changing body, mind, and spirit. Adopt healthy habits around sleep, nutrition, exercise, stress relief, and relationships. Treat yourself with compassion as you adapt to your new vessel.

Also, courageously share your struggles - whether physical, emotional, or social. No one figures this all out alone. Allow mentors who have walked before you to provide guidance when the path ahead seems uncertain. There is no weakness in asking for directions when lost.

Most importantly, maintain faith in your inner compass, that silent wisdom flowing within. Listen to your authentic voice, even if it whispers beneath the internal chatter and external noise. Let your unique spirit be the pilot light guiding your choices.

Of course, some days the turbulence will be more forceful. The key is not fighting the discomfort when it arises instead, acknowledge it with radical self-acceptance. Be the wise observer of your transformation, with a knowing that all is unfolding just as it should.

Your experiences during this passage, however messy, are awakening you to your deepest truths. So do not resist the ride - lean in to discover yourself anew. Mine each moment for the jewel of insight it offers. Allow this process of becoming to mold you into the luminous being you were destined to manifest as.

No butterfly ever lamented the struggles it took to break free of the cocoon that housed its growth. In time, you will look back on these temporary trials as stepping stones toward your fullest potential. For now, be gentle yet courageous in continuing onward.

Yes, the journey between adolescence and adulthood is often emotionally turbulent - but if navigated consciously can transport you to soaring new heights. Each challenge strengthens your metaphorical wings. You will soon fly higher than ever imagined!

So, breathe, trust, release, transform. We are all rooting for your ultimate blossoming into the majestic being you were born to be. Keep unveiling your glorious true colors. Take pride in this incredible adventure you are on.

Key Takeaways:

1. Understanding yourself is crucial during this transition phase.

2. Managing personal changes can be challenging but with effective strategies, it's manageable.

3. Expressing your needs and asking for help is not a sign of weakness but strength.

4. Navigating unsettled emotions is part of the process; seeking professional help when needed is important.

Chapter 2

Navigating Identity, Who Am I Now? Building Confidence and Self-Esteem as a Young Adult

I. Introduction

As you embark on your journey into adulthood, a robust sense of self-worth and belief in your abilities act as compass and fuel to guide your way. This chapter provides insights and strategies to help you cultivate iron-clad yet humble self-esteem and confidence.

I. The Critical Role of Self-Esteem and Confidence

A smooth transition into adulthood hinges on developing a healthy self-concept. Self-esteem refers to your subjective evaluation of self-worth and satisfaction with yourself overall. Confidence means faith in your competencies to handle situations and achieve aspirations.

Why are these fundamental? Self-esteem is the inner barometer that monitors your value. With high self-regard, you treat yourself kindly, reasonably believe you deserve happiness, and handle inevitable setbacks resiliently. Confidence allows you to approach unfamiliar or challenging territory courageously. It empowers you to spread your wings fully.

Conversely, those plagued by self-doubt often self-sabotage and cling to the familiar.

Lacking self-worth dims your inner light needed to illuminate adulthood's winding road ahead. Deficient confidence breeds hesitation. Robust self-esteem and confidence thus allow you to embrace adulthood as an adventure, not an ordeal.

The far-reaching benefits of healthy self-esteem have been demonstrated extensively through decades of research. The preventive benefits of building self-esteem earlier in life are clear. By developing self-compassion during your adolescence, you invest in decades of future happiness and fulfillment. Consider cultivating your self-worth during this transitional period of powerful preventative medicine for the mind, body, and soul throughout adulthood.

So, as you prepare to spread your wings, prioritize bolstering self-esteem and self-compassion. The journey into adulthood will have its inevitable ups and downs. But by laying this foundation, you equip yourself to handle challenges with poise and maximize opportunities with zeal.

II. Demystifying the Psychological Foundations (The Science of Self-Esteem and Confidence)

While loosely interconnected, self-esteem and confidence have distinct psychological underpinnings.

Self-Esteem: The Research of Dr. Morris Rosenberg

The pioneering researcher of self-esteem, Dr. Morris Rosenberg, defined it as a subjective self-assessment of one's worth based on qualities like self-respect, self-capability, and competence. Unlike arrogance or hubris, true self-esteem manifests as humble self-acceptance.

Confidence: The Role of Self-Efficacy

Confidence aligns closely with psychologist Albert Bandura's concept of self-efficacy - your belief that you can handle situations and accomplish goals with time and effort. Extensive studies show self-efficacy fuels motivation and perseverance in the face of challenges.

Both self-esteem and confidence levels ebb and flow throughout life as we accumulate successes and setbacks. Constructively processing each experience allows continual growth in self-concept over time. Core self-worth remains steady if you respond to stumbles with self-forgiveness.

Interconnected Yet Distinct

While linked, self-esteem and confidence differ subtly. You may exude confidence regarding certain domains like academics or sports but struggle with broader self-acceptance. Some highly accomplished individuals secretly feel like imposters.

The wisest path integrates self-esteem's roots with confidence's wings. Value your inherent worth while building tangible skills. Embrace your strengths and accept limitations gracefully. Let self-esteem water the soil for confidence to sprout and flourish.

III. Nurturing Self-Esteem and Confidence

As you traverse adulthood's obstacles, self-esteem provides a nurturing inner voice that muffles harsh critics fueled by fear. Confidence gives you the courage to lean into growth opportunities. Intentionally building both empowers you to realize your potential with zeal.

Here are golden principles and strategies for cultivating robust self-esteem and confidence:

The Anecdote of Lily

Lily was an aspiring artist who left home for college feeling incredibly insecure. Throughout childhood, her parents criticized her creative pursuits, pushing her toward more "practical" careers. Secretly painting brought Lily joy, but she lacked belief in her abilities.

At college, Lily isolated herself, avoiding classes where she would need to display her art publicly. She worked privately in her dorm room, destroying pieces that felt imperfect. Lily's inner critic berated her for pursuing such an unlikely career path given her lack of natural giftedness.

However, when a compassionate professor noticed Lily's absence and reached out, things began changing. He convinced her to just take one art class, gently reminding Lily that skill takes practice.

In class, Lily met fellow artists who welcomed her into their community. Their support, combined with the professor's encouragement, slowly emboldened her. She allowed herself to stop hiding her passion and started spending more time painting, without judgment, just for its inherent pleasure.

Gradually, Lily's technical abilities improved, along with her self-belief. Although she still felt anxious about displaying her art publicly, each small exhibition built her confidence. She began to appreciate her unique artistic voice.

By the time Lily graduated, she had displayed her work in several galleries. The constructively critical feedback helped her develop resilience. Lily found that when she focused on the intrinsic joy of creating, external validation mattered less. Her self-esteem now stemmed from doing what she loved.

Today, Lily continues honing her craft while proudly identifying as an artist. Though insecurities still occasionally surface, her inner light shines brighter, empowering her to withstand criticism. By daring to walk her own path, Lily learned she could quiet her inner critic and flourish.

IV. Discovering Your Authentic Self

A strong sense of identity provides sturdy roots for self-esteem and confidence to thrive. As you transition out of childhood roles, consciously defining your identity becomes critical. Childhood programmed beliefs about yourself may not align with who you genuinely are or aspire to become.

Your identity encompasses personality traits, values, interests, strengths, weaknesses, beliefs, cultural background, and life experiences that distinguish you as an individual. This multidimensional self-concept evolves throughout your life span as you accumulate knowledge and experiences.

Adolescence represents an ideal window to actively explore different aspects of identity. Allow yourself to play with potential identities, take personality assessments, identify passions, excavate your past, and listen to your inner wisdom. By diving below society's labels and programmed roles, you can resurface with a clearer vision of your authentic self.

Here are techniques to illuminate self-understanding:

Assess Personality and Temperament

Personality assessments like Myers-Briggs and Enneagram categorize inclination and temperament. Tests provide a vocabulary to articulate your innate dispositions. For instance, knowing whether you are introverted or extroverted allows self-acceptance and caters choices to meet your needs.

However, remember these tools offer general frameworks, not rigid edicts. Use results for self-insight, but do not let them limit your possibilities for growth. Your personality represents just one dimension of your multidimensional identity.

Uncover Your Passions and Talents

Make a list of activities that absorb you and bring deep satisfaction. When do you lose track of time because you enter a state of flow? Finding your niches of innate talent and passion reveals parts of yourself longing for expression. Carve out time to regularly engage these interests.

Some potential clues: the topics you could talk about for hours, creative pastimes you gravitate toward, fleeting childhood passions before practicality set in, online rabbit holes and searches, etc.

Let Values Guide You

Your values represent core principles and beliefs about life that shape priorities, ethics, and judgment. Reflect on questions like: What matters most to me? What do I believe is the purpose or meaning of life?

What principles guide my decisions? What legacy do I want to leave behind?

Uncover values that resonate then intentionally align choices with these convictions. This fosters integrity and direction. Be willing to shed values adopted from others that no longer fit.

Rewrite Your Story

Look back at impactful life experiences thus far. How have they shaped you? Appreciate all the people, challenges, and milestones that contributed to your growth. But also reflect on how limiting beliefs or narratives adopted in the past may not serve you moving forward.

For example, let go of excessive modesty or reticence if it inhibits pursuing your calling. Allow your present wisdom to revise past stories holding you back.

Trust Your Inner Voice

Solitude and stillness open a direct channel to your inner truth. Meditation and journaling reveal the subtle whispers of your authentic self, buried below internal noise. Give space for long-hidden aspects of your identity to gently rise and integrate.

By consistently checking in with your inner compass, you will gain clarity about who you genuinely are and want to become. Be patient with and curious about any self-resistance. Reconcile fragmented pieces into a coherent whole.

There Is No Fixed You

Core aspects of identity remain steady, but your self-concept will continue evolving. Avoid rigid labels. Stay open to discovering new dimensions of yourself as you grow. Be selectively permeable between ingrained aspects of your identity and potential areas still unexplored.

Allow this self-discovery process to gradually reveal your deepest truths. With courage, creativity and compassion, you will become who you were always meant to be.

V. Conclusion

In summary, this chapter provided essential guidance to help you have:

- An understanding of the psychological foundations of self-esteem and confidence. By exploring seminal research and theories behind self-concept, you can appreciate why nurturing self-worth and belief in your capabilities is so pivotal.

- An awareness of how critical robust self-esteem and confidence are as you embark on adulthood. Developing these inner resources helps you approach challenges resiliently and pursue dreams boldly.

- Tangible strategies to bolster your self-regard and self-belief. The anecdotes, assessments, and hands-on tips provided can be applied immediately to start strengthening your self-image.

- Tools for discovering your authentic identity and innate strengths. Clarifying your personality, values, interests, and skills empowers you to chart your unique course forward.

This knowledge lays the groundwork to spread your wings fully as you take flight into adulthood. Remember that self-discovery is a lifelong journey. With consistent courage, creativity, and compassion continue embracing your emerging self.

The future shimmers with possibility, awaiting the fuller expression of the wondrous being you were born to be. Believe in that light within you, and your wings will never falter.

Chapter 3

From Dependency to Autonomy: Developing Independence

I. Introduction

This is it! At this stage in life, you're trading in childhood's training wheels for the open road of adulthood, and that means freedom like you've never known. Exciting, right? But hold on, because with this sweet liberation comes a hefty chunk of responsibility too. Now, you're somewhat like the captain of your own ship, navigating finances, emotions, and all the social squalls life throws your way.

Remember those years under the watchful eyes of teachers and parents? Yeah, that safety net's about to vanish, replaced with a wide-open horizon – exhilarating and kind of terrifying all at once. But don't let the blank canvas freak you out! This is your chance to paint your masterpiece, and you've got the tools to do it. Master the art of responsibility – budget like a boss, manage your time like a magician, and make decisions that land you on top, not face-first in the dirt. With these superpowers, you'll grab life by the reins and steer it exactly where you want it to go. So, take a deep breath, trust your instincts, and get ready to conquer adulthood – it's your adventure to own!

Consider Jasmine, a 17-year-old embarking on her first year of college. After growing up in a protective household headed by strict parents who tightly regulated her activities, Jasmine finds herself overwhelmed by all the choices she must suddenly make alone about everything from course schedules to budgets. Initially excited by her new independence, she soon feels lost without external guidance. Jasmine squanders time, misses assignments, overspends her limited funds, and struggles to balance her demanding course load with her active social life. By the second semester of freshman year, Jasmine is on the verge of academic probation and financial crisis. She realizes that independence requires more than just the absence of rules. To gain true autonomy, Jasmine must cultivate personal accountability, discipline, and self-direction. Committing to daily planner use, budget tracking, and better decisions about priorities helps Jasmine finish the year strong, wiser for the challenges overcome.

Just like Jasmine, all young people eventually must transition from depending on caretakers to directing their own lives. Yet the skills deficit created by prolonged external control can undermine their success. As emerging adults, the ability to manage yourself, make sound choices, and handle responsibilities marks the difference between flailing and flourishing while adjusting to greater freedom. Cultivating critical independence competencies allows you to enjoy autonomy without feeling overwhelmed. Thus, this pivotal phase of development is an opportune time to instill such skills.

II. The Importance of Independence

Why should your independence matter so much in your transition to adulthood? Research links perceived autonomy to higher levels of psychological well-being across the lifespan (Ryan & Deci 2000). Self-sufficient young adults demonstrably fare better across measures of life satisfaction, purpose, and self-confidence.

You're on the cusp of adulthood when self-reliance unlocks possibility. I know shedding dependence feels daunting, but herein lies freedom: handling life yourself enables agency to steer your course.

Consider peers helpless without parental support, struggling to pursue passions. Then envision self-sufficient people accessing abundant opportunities through accountability.

The same truth applies to you. Adulthood's boundless freedom requires commensurate responsibility. Like driving, you cannot safely operate a vehicle without skillful control. As you shift into adulthood, cultivating competence powers your thrive.

So, embrace this transition to build essential life skills - lay the bricks of growth now. Discover confidence by claiming "I've got this" without a constant co-pilot. Trust your ability to chart your own passage ahead. Let self-rule allow your gifts to unfold.

III. Taking Responsibility: How to Accept & Learn from Mistakes

You're on the precipice of adulthood when responsibility matters. What does this truly mean? At its essence, it's owning outcomes rather than blaming external factors. This links to feeling in control of events through your behavior. This relates closely to the psychological concept of having an internal locus of control (Rotter 1966). When individuals believe they can influence events through their behavior, they operate from an internal locus.

Conversely, perceiving helplessness breeds an external locus where results seem wholly outside your power. This explains away missteps rather than extracting lessons. Yet self-accountability despite challenges is maturity.

Consider iconic figures like J.K. Rowling, rejected by publishers, or Jobs, fired from Apple. Both struggled enormously before succeeding. Rather than giving up, they looked inward at shortcomings, listened to feedback, and persevered.

Owning mistakes allows personal evolution. Studies reveal attitude toward failure predicts achievement more than IQ (Dweck 2006). Your still-developing brain makes emerging adulthood ripe for building responsibility through error learning. Missteps teach resilience and grit to accomplish hard things.

So how to internalize responsibility? First, reflect non-defensively on past mistakes - why things went wrong, decisions made, and consequences overlooked. This builds wisdom. Journal exercises can facilitate introspection. Unpack root causes from multiple angles.

Visualize alternative actions for better outcomes. Going forward, reframe missteps as feedback. When emotions like anxiety or embarrassment arise, actively calm feelings through slow breathing. Refocus analytically and extract insights. Discuss errors matter-of-factly with mentors to enrich perspectives.

Applying lessons breeds self-efficacy. Over time, mistakes become tools for growth rather than shame.

Note emotions arising when things go awry. Anger, embarrassment and anxiety signal avoidance coping (John & Gross 2004). You have the power to view responsibility as ownership, not blame. Mistakes will help you claim your adulthood.

IV. Time Management: Balancing School, Work, and Social Life

You're entering adulthood, suddenly juggling endless commitments. New realms bring multiplying demands - higher ed, jobs, social life, romance. Navigating these roles requires strategic time management.

Why critical? Efficiency enables achieving goals rather than overcommitting yet underachieving. A seminal study found adolescents with superior time management adapted better to adult roles later (Trueman & Hartley, 1996). Smooth adjustment requires organization, prioritization, and scheduling.

This doesn't come naturally. Hurdles like procrastination, underestimating time, and distractions lead to cramming and missed deadlines.

The good news is time management can be strengthened intentionally. Start tracking all obligations on a master calendar to visualize workload and catch bottlenecks. Thoughtfully schedule activities with buffers. Break projects into staged benchmarks. Generate prioritized daily to-do lists from the master schedule. This prevents getting sidetracked.

Also use helpful tools - planners, reminder apps and timers. Timebox tasks. Minimize digital distractions with website blockers when working. Most importantly, build consistency through habit. Diligent daily practice eases strain, gradually becoming routine.

You have the power to harness demands. With strategy, this landscape won't overwhelm but unlock. Streamline schedules to unfold potential.

V. Critical Decision-Making Skills: Making Informed Decisions

You're in emerging adulthood, facing major personal decisions with lasting impact - education, career, relationships, lifestyle choices. Navigating these high-stakes options responsibly demands discernment.

Mature decision-making capacity is a chief cognitive difference between adolescence and full adulthood. Brain structures governing complex deliberation continue developing into our mid-20s (Steinberg et al., 2018). This prolongs adolescent poor judgment, highlighting the need to build skills during this transitional period as neural networks strengthen.

Thoroughly considering alternatives aids clarity. Creative brainstorming sessions can uncover unconsidered directions. Trusted advisors widen perspectives.

Next, weigh the pros and cons of each path against goals using tools like decision matrices. Research outcomes realistically, accounting for probability and time. Envision distant targets already fulfilled to guide present action toward them. Core values provide standards for evaluating tradeoffs.

Dilute emotions by postponing complicated decisions temporarily. Revisit with fresh eyes later, often shifting perspective. Sleep clears intensity enabling a balanced cost-benefit analysis. If high-stakes choices get overshadowed by momentary drama or desire, delay allows passion to cool so the best path signals itself.

Questions prompting rational reasoning include: What are quantifiable costs and benefits? Who does this impact short and long-term? What assumptions underlie my analysis? What meaningful data do I lack? Am I overvaluing unimportant preferences? Are biases shaping my thinking?

Consider best- and worst-case scenarios across possibilities. Assess readiness for various trajectories regarding responsibilities, effort, and sacrifices. Reviewing past pivotal decisions illustrates growth and offers future insight. Older mentors expose expanded considerations. Synthesize these diverse inputs to construct clarity.

After thorough reflection, identify the optimal path aligning with your core values and enriching long-term purpose. Commit fully, upholding perseverance until the choice bears fruit. Revisit evaluations periodically given new input.

Independent well-informed decisions are ongoing work amidst profound identity development. However, consistently applying critical thinking and analysis allows self-directed maturity. Just as physical exertion builds muscle, regularly exercising discernment develops intuition and sound judgment to guide your journey.

VI. Conclusion

The emergence of autonomy marks a pivotal milestone of the winding road into adulthood. Though the initial taste of newfound freedom beckons excitingly, self-directedness raises vital skills development to properly support increasing independence. As the preceding discussion illuminated, cultivating personal responsibility, time management, and critical decision-making abilities empower young people to direct their own lives successfully.

While adversity inevitably arises on the path to self-sufficiency, perseverant effort focused on building competence breeds resilience to weather challenges with poise. Youth still unsure of how to take ownership of their futures should take heart that independence emerges intentionally through prioritizing the growth of agency. Applying lessons from mistakes instead of avoidance coping gradually strengthens the capability to handle difficulties with resourcefulness. Similarly, progress manifests through inducing small wins in managing time and choices via incremental discipline aimed at gathering wisdom over time. Maturity appears not necessarily chronologically but behaviorally as emerging adults learn navigating life's maze relies on self-accountability.

The quest of discovering one's best self, calls for proactivity, initiative and grit rather than passive waiting for answers to materialize spontaneously. Young people owe it to their highest potential to seize their ripening autonomy as an opportunity to develop self-trust through repeatedly facing the fire of demanding trials and rising stronger for it. In doing so, the path ahead ultimately unveils itself through a steadfast rhythm of living one's truths. May all youth embrace their blossoming independence as a privilege in the promise of expanding freedom and dedicate their energies toward unlocking their best lives equipped with the essential inner resources illuminated through these pages. The future shines bright for emerging adults prepared to chart their own course. Here's to embarking on that worthy voyage of self-discovery!

Key Takeaways:

• Taking responsibility for choices rather than blaming others enables learning from mistakes which fosters growth through resilience.

• Managing competing demands on time prevents overload and allows achieving goals in education, careers, and relationships by planning, prioritizing, and maintaining focus.

• Making fully informed decisions aligned with personal values through discovery of options, critical evaluation, and reasoned reflection boosts agency over life direction.

Exercises:

• Journal about past mistakes without self-judgment and consider alternative paths forward

• Create master schedule reflecting key commitments then design an effective daily to-do list system

• Brainstorm pros/cons list of a current complex personal decision, identify information gaps, short and long-term impacts to determine optimal choice

Chapter 4

Personal Development: Have a Resilient Growth Mindset

I. Introduction

As you embark on the journey of adulthood, actively focusing on personal growth and self-improvement will serve you tremendously. Cultivating resilience and a growth mindset are key in handling the inevitable challenges and setbacks that life presents. This chapter provides practical strategies to develop essential resources to thrive amid adversity.

We first explore the critical skill of resilience - the capacity to recover quickly from difficulties. Through real-world stories and evidence-based steps, you'll learn how to build resilience to weather storms. Next, we unpack the transformative power of adopting a growth mindset, the belief that abilities can be developed through dedication and effort. Integrating these mindsets lays the foundation for fulfillment and success. Equipped with an understanding of resilience and growth, you can craft a vision for your future and map steps to achieve dreams.

You'll discover how research-backed techniques from leading psychology experts equip you to thrive through difficult periods and achieve greatness by unleashing your talents incrementally.

II. Understanding Resilience

Simply put, resilience refers to coping well under stress or crisis. It means effectively navigating setbacks, challenges, adversity or trauma and bouncing back in a flexible, adaptive way. Resilience isn't an innate fixed trait though - scientists believe behaviors supporting resilience can intentionally be built up, fortifying this vital skill over time.

Research by positive psychology pioneer Dr. Martin Seligman found that resilience correlates with signature strengths of courage, optimism, self-control, responsibility and perseverance. Studies show resilience bolsters both physical and mental health. It also enhances performance by enabling cool-headed decision making amid chaos. Luckily, we can reinforce our resilience reserves through shifting ingrained thought patterns and doubling down on positive habits.

In the sweltering heat of 1962 California, a young woman named Bethany Hamilton dreamt of conquering the waves. At just 13 years old, Bethany was already a rising star in the world of amateur surfing, with a natural talent and infectious enthusiasm. Then, on Halloween morning, everything changed.

While paddling off Tunnels Beach on Maui, Bethany encountered a 14-foot tiger shark. In a terrifying instant, the shark attacked, severing her left arm between the shoulder and elbow. Blood pouring into the turquoise water, Bethany clung to her surfboard, her screams echoing across the bay. Her friends, surfers Alana Blanchard and Sarah Ludington, bravely paddled closer and helped drag her to shore.

Bethany's world had been ripped apart. She faced the unimaginable - the loss of a limb, the end of her surfing dreams, and the daunting prospect of navigating life with a permanent disability. Yet, from the hospital bed, Bethany showed a remarkable spark of resilience. Instead of succumbing to despair, she focused on what she could still do. She learned to surf again, adapting her technique to her new reality. Within months, she was back on the water, riding waves with a prosthetic arm and an even stronger determination.

But Bethany's journey wasn't just about conquering physical challenges. She faced intense public scrutiny, becoming a media sensation both for her tragic accident and her inspiring comeback. She grappled with self-doubt and fear, the whispers of "what if" playing on repeat in her mind. Yet, Bethany chose to see her experience as a platform for good. She founded the Bethany Hamilton Foundation, advocating for amputees and inspiring others to overcome adversity.

Fast forward to today, Bethany's story is an international beacon of resilience. She has won numerous surfing competitions, including the ESPY Award for Best Comeback Athlete. She's a global spokesperson for amputee rights, traveling the world to share her story and empower others. Bethany's spirit shines through in her infectious smile, her determination to defy limitations, and her unwavering belief that even the fiercest storms can't extinguish the fire within.

Bethany Hamilton's story is more than just a real-life example of resilience; it's a testament to the human spirit's ability to rise above and rewrite the narrative. It's a reminder that even when the waves crash down, there's always the possibility of riding them to victory. Remember, just like Bethany, you too possess the strength to overcome any obstacle life throws your way. You just need to find your board, paddle out, and face the waves with courage and a resilient heart.

III. Building Your Own Resilience

Now let's get hands-on with concrete methods for cultivating greater resilience in your own life. By implementing these proven self-care strategies and self-reflection exercises deliberately each day, you reinforce resilience bit by bit like building sturdy scaffolding. Consider adding a few of these tactics progressively until they become automated routine:

Stress Management 101

- Prioritize proper sleep, nutrition, hydration

- Exercise, yoga, mindfulness meditation

- Nature walks, social connection

- Laughing, humor, optimistic thinking

Emotional Agility Training

- Allow yourself to fully feel emotions during adversity or change

- Then use inner dialogue to self-soothe, gain perspective

- Unpack fears, reframe situations realistically

Self-Care & Routine

- Set manageable goals each day

- Check off small task wins, track progress

- Practice regular self-compassion breaks

Growth Mindset Reconditioning

- Notice fixed mindset self-talk during challenges

- Consciously shift inner voice to growth narrative

- Recall past successes overcoming obstacles

Leverage Support Systems

- Open up to trusted confidant about difficulties

- Seek counseling or support groups if needed

- Give and receive encouragement

By integrating small, resilient thoughts and behaviors into your wheelhouse, you build the muscle memory required to handle adversity smoothly when those wasting punches do inevitably come. The potent combination of resting self-compassion while maintaining realistic optimism, self-efficacy and social connection primes you to get back up time and again.

IV. Understanding Growth Mindset

Now that we've reinforced resilience foundations, let's level up one more essential personal growth skill - cultivating a growth mindset. This concept stemmed from the transformative research of Stanford psychologist Dr. Carol Dweck demonstrating that people's core assumptions about learning and talent dictated their capacity for success.

Specifically, Dr. Dweck's studies revealed two different frameworks people operated from regarding their abilities. Those with a fixed mindset believe talents are set innately at birth. Since they view aptitudes as fixed, they frequently experience helplessness in the face of struggle, avoiding growth opportunities that risk failure. On the other hand, people holding a growth-oriented mindset see talents as flexible processes that can be built incrementally through practice. They interpret challenges as feedback driving mastery, allowing them to achieve exponentially more over decades.

The good news? Decades of compelling research prove that embodying a growth narrative is a teachable skill open to anyone simply by reshaping habitual thought patterns. When you consciously reinforce self-talk and behaviors matching your talents as always a work in progress, you prime yourself for success through tenacious, resilient effort. Let's discover how to continually tap into your special sauce of human potential through the incremental growth approach.

V. Cultivating Your Growth Mindset

Operating from a growth mindset is about embracing self-improvement over searching for fixed validation. View challenges as fuel to expand your capabilities through building knowledge, talents, and wisdom over time. Set learning-oriented goals to build skills, collecting small wins systematically toward eventual mastery.

Persisting through inevitable setbacks also forges grit and resilience while disempowering sabotaging thoughts claiming tasks impossible. Replace self-limiting narratives with constructive feedback and varied solution testing until a breakthrough sticks. Assess efforts accurately and acknowledge areas for targeted improvement to support incremental progress strategically.

For inspiration, examine (example) overcoming odds through tireless work ethic, hunger for continuous advancement and blocking out naysayers with self-belief. Let nothing deter you from progressing closer to fulfilling potential, even if by tiny leaps when major bounds feel beyond reach initially. With consistent effort allocated wisely each day, small steps compound into great leaps over months and years.

Strategies to develop growth mindset:

- View challenges as opportunities

- Persist through setbacks

- Replace self-defeating talk

- Seek input to improve

- Try innovative solutions

The remarkable story of Vincent van Gogh, an artist whose journey embodies the power of a growth mindset. Imagine the late 19th century, France. Vincent, a struggling art dealer longing for artistic expression, finds himself at 27, jobless and directionless. With no formal training and being ridiculed by critics, his early attempts at painting are deemed amateurish and dark. He even suffers a mental breakdown in 1889.

This could have been the end, the narrative sealed. But Vincent, fueled by a relentless growth mindset, refused to let limitations define him. He embraced his setbacks as opportunities to learn. He tirelessly absorbed influences from fellow artists like Gauguin and Seurat, experimenting with new techniques and styles. Even amidst financial hardship and emotional turmoil, he painted fervently, pouring his heart and soul onto canvas.

Take Van Gogh's infamous "Starry Night," now a masterpiece celebrated worldwide. Painted in 1889 while residing in the Saint-Paul asylum, it wasn't initially met with acclaim. Critics considered its swirling brushstrokes and vibrant colors chaotic and unsettling. Yet, Vincent saw it as a breakthrough, a representation of his inner turmoil and profound connection to the natural world. He remained undeterred by criticism, continuing to evolve his style and push the boundaries of artistic expression.

The results are undeniable. Over a decade of unwavering dedication, Vincent produced over 2,100 artworks, including iconic landscapes, portraits, and still-life images. Though he never witnessed his commercial success during his lifetime, his relentless pursuit of growth laid the foundation for his posthumous recognition as one of the greatest artists of all time.

Here's what makes Vincent's story such a potent example of a growth mindset:

Embracing Challenges: He saw setbacks and criticism as learning opportunities, constantly evolving his technique and style.

Seeking New Knowledge: He actively studied the works of other artists, readily absorbing influences and experimenting with new ideas.

Resilience in the Face of Doubt: He remained unwavering in his artistic vision, unfazed by initial rejection and financial hardship.

Continuous Learning: He treated every canvas as a chance to grow, honing his craft and pushing the boundaries of artistic expression.

Van Gogh's story doesn't just chronicle artistic brilliance; it's a testament to the transformative power of a growth mindset. It reminds us that even in the face of adversity, with dedicated effort and a willingness to learn and evolve, we can paint our own masterpieces, whatever your chosen field may be.

So, the next time you face a challenge or doubt your abilities, remember Van Gogh's unwavering spirit. Embrace the opportunity to learn and grow, and never stop painting your own masterpiece, one brushstroke at a time.

VI. Goal Setting

Goals are Your Secret Weapon for Personal Growth.

Imagine navigating a vast, uncharted ocean without a compass or destination. That's what life can feel like without goals. Setting goals is your guiding star, propelling you forward with purpose and direction. It is the fuel that ignites your motivation, the map that keeps you on track, and the anchor that steadies you through choppy waters.

So, why exactly is setting goals so crucial for personal development? Here are a few key reasons:

1. Clarity and Focus: Goals give you a laser-sharp vision of what you want to achieve. They transform vague aspirations into concrete objectives, helping you prioritize your time and energy toward what truly

matters. No more feeling lost or scattered—your goals give you a roadmap to follow.

2. Motivation and Drive: A well-defined goal is like a delicious carrot dangled before a horse. It keeps you energized and moving forward, pushing you to overcome obstacles and persevere through challenges. The closer you get to achieving your goal, the sweeter the reward, fueling your determination even further.

3. Increased Confidence: Accomplishing goals, big or small, instills a powerful sense of self-belief. Each milestone conquered is a testament to your abilities, boosting your confidence and paving the way for even greater aspirations. As you witness your own progress, you'll realize that anything is possible with dedication and the right plan.

4. Continuous Learning and Growth: Setting goals forces you to step outside your comfort zone and explore new territories. Whether it's learning a new skill, mastering a challenging task, or tackling a personal fear, your goals push you to grow and evolve, expanding your horizons and refining your skill set.

5. Improved Decision-Making: Goals act as a filter, helping you make choices that align with your desired

outcomes. When faced with multiple options, you can evaluate them through the lens of your goals, ensuring that each decision takes you closer to your ultimate destination.

Now that you're convinced of the power of goal setting let's dive into the practicalities! Enter the world of SMART goals – your key to transforming aspirations into actionable plans.

Remember: SMART stands for Specific, Measurable, Achievable, Relevant, and Time-bound. Let's break down each element:

Specific: Don't aim for generalities like "get healthy." Instead, pinpoint exactly what you want to achieve. For example, "run a 5K race within six months" is a specific goal.

Measurable: How will you track your progress? Quantify your goal with concrete metrics. In our 5K example, measurable markers could be weekly training distances or timed practice runs.

Achievable: Set goals that are challenging but attainable. Aim too high, and you risk discouragement; aim too low, and you might miss out on your full potential. Find that sweet spot where you feel stretched but confident.

Relevant: Ensure your goals align with your values, interests, and overall life vision. A 5K might be great for one person, but for another, mastering a musical instrument might be more relevant. Choose goals that resonate with you.

Time-bound: Give your goals a deadline! Without a timeframe, they can float around indefinitely. Set a specific date or period for achieving your goal, like "run the 5K on May 1st."

Incorporating these SMART principles transforms your goals from vague wishes into actionable blueprints for success. Remember, goal setting is an ongoing process. Regularly revisit your goals, adjust them as needed, and celebrate your milestones along the way. With dedication and the right plan, you'll be amazed at what you can achieve!

So, set sail on your personal development journey with the wind of well-defined goals at your back. Embrace the clarity, motivation, and growth that come with having a target in sight. Remember, the only limit is your own imagination – so dream big, set

SMART goals, and watch yourself conquer the uncharted waters of your potential!

VII. Health & Well-being 101

Hey you! Put down that third bag of chips (we'll follow up on healthier snacks) and prep for a quest of epic proportions: hacking your way to well-being. No mystical potions or mythical creatures involved – just you, your awesome body, and three secret weapons: physical activity, proper diet, and regular check-ups.

Why Move it, Move it?

Think of exercise as your personal hype squad, cheering you on to a healthier, happier you. But it's not just about sculpted bods (although, yeah, those are pretty cool too). Here's how movement becomes your superpower:

- Energy Explosion: Feeling like a deflated balloon? Exercise pumps up your energy levels, sending oxygen and endorphins on a victory lap through your body. Ditch the caffeine jitters and embrace the natural energy high that comes with getting your groove on.

- Stress Slayer: Life throws you curveballs, but with exercise, you can hit them out of the park. It's like a stress-melting superpower, calming your mind and body, and leaving you feeling Zen AF. Imagine conquering deadlines and social awkwardness with a warrior's calm – exercise can make that happen.

- Brain Power Booster: Exercise isn't just for your muscles; it's a workout for your brain, too! It enhances memory, focus, and cognitive function, turning you into a sharper, more productive version of yourself. Ace that exam, nail that presentation – your brain will be thanking you for those squats.

- Sleep Symphony: Tossing and turning like a pinball in a cosmic game? Exercise can be your lullaby. Regular physical activity regulates your sleep cycle, helping you drift off faster and sleep more soundly. Imagine waking up feeling like a well-rested superhero, ready to conquer the day – that's the power of movement.

- Happy Heart: Exercise strengthens your heart, improves circulation, and keeps your blood pressure in check. It's like giving your cardiovascular system a high five, keeping it ticking happily for the long haul. Think: fewer doctor visits, more epic adventures – exercise is your ticket to a healthy heart party.

Fueling Your Biohacking Engine

Food isn't just sustenance; it's the code that programs your temple's performance. Choose wisely, and you'll create a vibrant, high-functioning masterpiece. Ditch the junk food and embrace these biohacking fuel sources:

- Go Green Team: Load up on fruits, vegetables, and whole grains. These are nature's powerhouses, packed with vitamins, minerals, and fiber that keep your body running smoothly. Think of them as your daily dose of sunshine and rainbows for internal systems.

- Hydration Hero: Water is the elixir of life (seriously, though)! It keeps your body lubricated, your skin glowing, and your brain buzzing. Aim for eight glasses a day and watch your temple radiate health and vitality.

Imagine glowing like a human sunbeam –
hydration is your key.

- Protein Power: Protein is your body's building
  block, essential for muscle repair, growth, and
  feeling full. Lean meats, fish, legumes, and nuts
  are your protein pals, keeping you energized
  and ready for action. Think: conquering
  workouts, slaying deadlines, and feeling
  awesome – protein fuels your biohacking
  engine.

- Sugar Smackdown: Sugar is the sneaky villain
  in disguise. It spikes your blood sugar, leaving
  you feeling drained and craving more. Choose
  natural sugars from fruits and limit processed
  sugary treats. Your body (and taste buds) will
  thank you for ditching the sugar crash and
  embracing sustained energy.

- Mindful Munching: Pay attention to your
  body's hunger cues. Don't mindlessly graze;
  savor each bite and stop when you're
  comfortably full. This mindful approach helps
  you avoid overeating and tune into your body's
  needs. Think: becoming a biohacking Jedi,

listening to your inner wisdom and fueling your temple with intention.

Doctor Date, Don't Debate:

Regular check-ups aren't just for when you're feeling under the weather. They're like preventive maintenance for your temple, catching potential issues early and keeping you on track for optimal health. Here's why they're crucial:

- Early Detection: Regular check-ups can detect potential health problems early on, when they're easier to treat and manage. Think of it as a map that helps you navigate any bumps in the road before they become mountains. No one wants to deal with unexpected health dramas – be proactive and get those check-ups!

- Preventative Care: Vaccinations, screenings, and lifestyle advice can help prevent chronic diseases and keep your body strong and resilient. It's like investing in a force field to protect your temple from harm. Think: avoiding future health battles and staying on top of your game – regular check-ups are your secret weapon.

- Personalized Plan: Your doctor is your health partner, working with you to create a personalized plan that fits your unique needs and goals. They'll be your cheerleader, your advisor, and your guide on your well-being journey. Imagine having a health Yoda in your corner – that's what your doctor can be!

- Peace of Mind: Worried about niggling symptoms? Regular check-ups can ease your anxiety and provide clarity. Think: ditching the stress of unknowns and getting answers to keep your mind peaceful and focused on your adventures.

Weaving Wellness into Your Life:

Now, let's ditch the daunting and embrace the doable! Here are some tips to seamlessly integrate these habits into your daily life:

- Move it, Move it: Find activities you genuinely enjoy – dancing, cycling, rock climbing, even brisk walks with friends. Start small and gradually increase intensity and duration. Remember, every step counts!

- Fuel Your Engine: Keep healthy snacks like fruits, nuts, and veggies handy for on-the-go munching. Plan your meals with colorful veggies and lean protein sources. Don't demonize treats – enjoy them mindfully and in moderation.

- Doctor Dates: Schedule regular check-ups and proactive screenings based on your age and health risks. Don't hesitate to voice any concerns you have – your doctor is there to listen and guide you.

VIII. Conclusion:

Remember, well-being isn't about perfection; it's about progress. Celebrate your victories, learn from setbacks, and keep biohacking your way to a healthier, happier you. Your body is your temple, your playground, your instrument – treat it with love, respect, and a healthy dose of fun. Now go forth, brave adventurer, and conquer your own well-being quest!

Activities/Exercises:

- Movement Challenge: Choose a physical activity you've always wanted to try and commit to it for a week. Document your experience and share it with friends for extra motivation.

- Food Journal: Track your food intake for a few days to understand your current eating patterns. Identify areas for improvement and set achievable goals for healthier choices.

- Doctor Dialogue: Write down any questions or concerns you have about your health and schedule a check-up with your doctor to discuss them openly.

- Biohacking Vision Board: Create a visual representation of your well-being goals, including healthy habits, desired outcomes, and inspirational quotes. Refer to it regularly to stay motivated and on track.

Remember, your well-being journey is your own. Embrace the joy of experimentation, personalize the strategies to fit your lifestyle, and most importantly, have fun in the process! Your healthier, happier you, awaits.

In review, resilience enables overcoming adversity while a growth mindset empowers achievement.

Research shows both can be strengthened through introducing positive personal development strategies.

Chapter 5

Crafting an Impressive Resume & Cover Letter and Nailing that Job Interview

I. Introduction

You've conquered the academic jungle, graduation gown flapping in the wind, diploma clutched in hand. Now, you stand at the threshold of the real world, eyes wide with anticipation and maybe a hint of job-hunting anxiety. Fear not, brave adventurer!

This chapter is your arsenal for crafting an epic resume and cover letter, then slaying that interview dragon and landing your dream job.

Think of your resume and cover letter as your personal hype squad and VIP pass to the career kingdom. They're the first impression you make on potential employers, the magic carpets transporting you to interview land, and the secret weapons that showcase your awesomeness. Crafting them well isn't just about ticking boxes; it's about storytelling, self-advocacy, and convincing people you're the missing piece to their professional puzzle.

II. Understanding Your Strengths, Skills, and Interests

Before you whip out your resume pen, a treasure hunt is in order! It's time to discover your own hidden talents, honed skills, and passions that can light up any workplace. Here's how to embark on this self-discovery quest:

- Strengths Safari: Write down everything you're good at, from communication skills to organizational superpowers. Don't be shy – list even seemingly quirky strengths like creativity, empathy, or problem-solving prowess.

- Skills Scavenger Hunt: Think about activities at which you excel, both academic and extracurricular. Did you lead a project team? Code a video game? Volunteer at an animal shelter? These experiences translate into valuable skills!

- Passion Pit Stop: What makes your heart sing? Whether it's writing, data analysis, or building sustainable houses, your passions can fuel your career journey and point you toward fulfilling jobs.

Exercise: Grab a sheet of paper and divide it into three sections: Strengths, Skills, and Interests. List at least five entries in each section. Now, try connecting the dots! Can your strength in communication be combined with your writing skills to land a copywriting job? Can your passion for sustainability and your data analysis skills lead to a role in green tech? Remember, the secret sauce lies in weaving your unique tapestry of strengths, skills, and interests to create a compelling job-hunting narrative.

III. Researching Potential Jobs

Now that you know your own magic, it's time to find the kingdom where it can shine. Researching potential jobs is like exploring a vast map – exciting, overwhelming, and full of hidden gems. Here's your compass:

- Strengths + Skills + Interests = Job Paradise: Use your self-discovery findings to target industries and roles that align with your unique talents and passions. Don't just follow the herd; chase the jobs that make your inner geek do a happy dance.

- Go Online, Young Adventurer: Websites like LinkedIn and Indeed are your treasure troves of job postings. Filter by keywords, location, and industry to create a personalized job hunt adventure. Research company websites and read industry news to get a feel for the job landscape.

- Network Like a Ninja: Talk to friends, family, and mentors who work in fields that interest you. Attend industry events or career fairs to connect with professionals and get insider tips. Remember, your network is your secret weapon, so treat it with respect and nurture it well.

IV. Crafting an Impressive Resume

A resume isn't just a laundry list of experiences; it's a compelling story of your professional journey. The first impression can land you an interview, so let's make it sing!

First Things First:

- Types of Resumes: There are three main types – chronological (highlights work experience in reverse order), functional (focuses on skills and abilities), and combination (blends both elements). Choose the one that best showcases your strengths and experience for the specific job you're applying for.

- Contact Information: Make sure your name, email address, and phone number are prominent and easy to find. Don't leave recruiters playing detective!

- Goal Statement: Craft a brief, attention-grabbing sentence that summarizes your career aspirations and aligns with the job you're applying for. Think of it as your professional elevator pitch.

Work Experience:

- Action Verbs are Your Friends: Ditch the boring "responsible for" phrases and spice things up with action verbs like "managed," "led," "organized," or "created." Quantify your achievements whenever possible. Did you increase sales by 15%? Managed a team of 10?

Make it measurable and impressive

Let's Make Your Work Experience Sparkle!

Quantify & Qualify: Numbers are your allies in the resume game. Did you boost website traffic by 20%? Did your research contribute to a 5% cost reduction? Highlight these achievements with hard data to showcase your impact. Remember, even seemingly small contributions can be quantified with creativity.

Focus on Achievements, Not Just Duties: Don't just list your responsibilities at past jobs. Describe specific projects you led, skills you used, and problems you solved. This could include volunteer or internship work you have done. Show, don't tell – let your accomplishments speak for themselves!

Tailor, Tailor, Tailor: Don't send the same generic resume for every job. Take the time to tailor your work experience section to the specific requirements and keywords listed in the job posting. Demonstrate how your past experiences directly relate to the skills and qualifications the employer is seeking.

Education Background:

- List your educational qualifications, including the name of the institution, degree earned, and relevant coursework, if applicable. Don't forget to mention any awards or scholarships you received that showcase your academic excellence.

- If you're a recent graduate, consider highlighting relevant projects, research experiences, or extracurricular activities that demonstrate your initiative and transferable skills.

Skills & Abilities:

- This is your chance to showcase your diverse skill set, from technical skills like coding or data analysis to soft skills like communication, teamwork, and problem-solving. Use keywords from the job posting and be specific about your level of proficiency.

- Consider including additional sections like volunteer work, language skills, or relevant certifications to further impress potential employers.

Pro Tips for Resume Awesomeness:

- Keep it Concise: Aim for one or two pages, depending on your experience level. Recruiters have short attention spans, so make your resume easy to scan and digest.

- Formatting Matters: Use clear fonts, headings, and bullet points for easy readability. Don't be afraid to add some white space to avoid a cluttered look.

- Proofread, Proofread, Proofread: Typos and grammatical errors are resume deal-breakers. Make sure your resume is error-free and polished before sending it out.

- Save it Wisely: Save your resume in a format that recruiters can easily access, like PDF or Word document. Consider having a separate online resume profile, like on LinkedIn, to expand your reach.

Remember, your resume is a living document that should evolve as your career progresses. Keep it updated with new skills, experiences, and relevant achievements. Most importantly, let your personality shine through! A genuine and enthusiastic resume can stand out from the crowd and land you that coveted interview.

V. Writing an Effective Cover Letter

You've crafted a resume that stands out, but you're not done yet. It's time to unleash your inner wordsmith and write a cover letter that takes your application to the next level. Think of it as your resume's hype squad, a personalized plea that convinces recruiters you're the missing piece to their professional puzzle.

Cover Letter Craft 101

So, what exactly is this magical document? A cover letter is your chance to bridge the gap between your resume and the hiring manager's mind. It's where you go beyond bullet points and tell a compelling story about why you're the perfect fit for the job. It's like a handshake across email or snail mail, showcasing your personality, enthusiasm, and specific skills relevant to the company and position.

Essential Elements:

- Salutations: Ditch the robotic "Dear Sir/Madam." Research the hiring manager's name and use it (bonus points for finding their LinkedIn profile and tailoring your opening to something they've posted!).

- Hook 'em with the First Line: Don't waste space on generic introductions. Start with a captivating sentence that highlights a shared interest, impressive achievement, or unique perspective on the company or role.

- Body Paragraphs: Skills on Parade: Explain why you're interested in the job and company. Showcase specific skills and experiences from your resume that directly align with the job requirements. Use the STAR method (Situation, Task, Action, Result) to tell impactful stories about your past successes.

- Call to Action: Don't be shy! End with a clear call to action, whether it's requesting an interview, expressing your willingness to provide additional information, or simply thanking them for their time.

Personalization Potion:

Remember, cookie-cutter cover letters are a recipe for disaster. Each application needs a dash of personalization to stand out. Here's how to brew the perfect potion:

- Keyword Alchemy: Sprinkle keywords from the job description throughout your letter. Show the recruiter you've actually read the posting and understand what they're looking for.

- Company Research Elixir: Immerse yourself in the company's website, social media, and news articles. This knowledge allows you to tailor your message to their values and mission, proving you're not just applying to any job.

- Passion Infusion: Don't be afraid to let your passion for the industry or company shine through. Show genuine enthusiasm and convince them you're not just chasing a paycheck.

VI. Acing Job Interviews – Dos and Don'ts:

So, you've landed the interview! This is not the time to doubt yourself. Ensure you channel your inner strength. Let's demystify the interview process and turn you into a confident conversationalist.

Understanding the Beast:

Interviews come in different flavors: phone screenings, face-to-face chats, group interviews, even video calls. Regardless of the format, their purpose is the same: for the company to assess your skills, personality, and cultural fit. Be prepared to flex your communication muscles and show them you're the real deal.

Preparation is Power:

Don't waltz into an interview unprepared. Research the company, industry, and specific role. Practice answering common interview questions (we'll get to those in a sec!), prepare questions for the interviewer, and plan your outfit (professional, not party!). Dress to impress, arrive early (but not too early – stalking is not a good look), and bring copies of your resume and references.

Question Quest:

Interviews are two-way streets. Be ready to answer a variety of questions, from behavioral ("Tell me about a time you...") to situational ("How would you handle...?"). Remember, STAR is your friend! Use it to showcase your problem-solving skills, teamwork abilities, and initiative. Don't be afraid to ask insightful questions too – it shows you're genuinely interested in the company and the role.

The Dos and Don'ts of Interview Awesomeness:

- Do: Maintain eye contact, smile, and project confidence. Show genuine enthusiasm and be polite to everyone you encounter.

- Don't: Badmouth past employers, fidget, or speak negatively about yourself. Avoid slang and unprofessional language.

- Bonus Tip: Prepare a closing statement that summarizes your key skills and reiterates your interest in the job. Leave a lasting impression that screams, "Hire me!"

Common Interview Questions, Conquered:

- "Tell me about yourself." This is your chance to craft a concise elevator pitch that highlights your skills and career goals. Focus on what's relevant to the job and keep it personal.

- "Why are you interested in this position?" Do your research! Demonstrate your knowledge of the company's mission and values, and explain how your skills and experience align with their needs.

- "Tell me about a time you faced a challenge..." Use the STAR method to share a story about a problem you solved, highlighting your decision-making skills, communication abilities, and ability to overcome obstacles.

- "What are your salary expectations?" Research the average salary range for the position and location. Be confident and realistic in your response, and be open to negotiation.

- "Do you have any questions for me?" This is your chance to shine! Ask thoughtful questions about the company culture, team dynamics, and your potential responsibilities. Show genuine interest and proactive curiosity.

VII. The Power of Networking

The job market isn't just about resumes and interviews, it's about connections. Networking is like planting seeds that can blossom into unexpected opportunities. Here's how to build your professional garden:

- Go Offline: Attend industry events, conferences, and workshops. Join professional organizations and volunteer for relevant causes. Strike up conversations, build relationships, and learn from experienced professionals.

- Embrace Online: LinkedIn is your digital networking paradise. Connect with people in your field, participate in group discussions, and showcase your expertise. Share valuable content and engage with relevant communities.

- Don't Be Shy: Ask friends, family, and former colleagues for referrals or introductions. Don't be afraid to reach out to professionals you admire – you never know what doors might open.

VIII. Conclusion

Landing your dream job isn't always a straight shot. It takes patience, persistence, and a healthy dose of self-belief. Keep honing your skills, refining your application materials, and actively networking. The right opportunity will come your way, and when it does, you'll be ready to grab it with confidence.

Remember, the skills you learn in this chapter aren't just for landing your first job – they're for navigating your entire career journey. Keep your resume and cover letter arsenal polished, sharpen your interview skills, and cultivate your professional network. You've got this, adventurer! Now, go forth and conquer the job market!

Key Takeaways:

- A well-crafted cover letter complements your resume and increases your chances of landing an interview.

- Effective job interview skills, from preparation to answering questions confidently, are crucial for success.

- Building a strong professional network can open doors to hidden opportunities.

- Patience, persistence, and continuous learning are key to achieving your career goals.

Exercises/Activities:

- Write a mock cover letter for a specific job posting.

- Practice answering common interview questions using the STAR method.

- Conduct a mock interview with a friend or family member.

- Connect with five new people on LinkedIn who work in your field of interest.

Remember, the more you practice, the more confident you'll become. So, don't wait – start applying these strategies today and watch your career dreams take flight!

Part II:

Managing Your Finances in the Adult World

Chapter 6:

Money Matters Basics - Mastering the Game of Your Personal Finances

I. Introduction

Remember the rush of landing your first job? That sweet paycheck is a symbol of independence and freedom. But hold on, money adventurer, the real journey is just beginning! Financial literacy, the art of understanding and managing your finances, is your crucial companion in this quest.

Imagine Chloe, your college buddy, landing a fantastic gig. Money seemed to rain down ceaselessly– trendy gadgets, gourmet coffee dates, weekend getaways galore came easy. Savings? Non-existent. Then, life threw a quick jab at her. Car breakdowns, medical bills, a surprise career shift... Chloe's financial oasis turned into a desert, leaving her scrambling for scraps. Don't let this be your story, dear friend!

This chapter is your Rosetta Stone, decoding the mysteries of money and transforming you into a financial ninja. First things first: income, the fuel that powers your financial engine. It comes in flavors: active income you earn from your job, passive income like rent or investment returns, and the hidden gem called portfolio income from stocks, bonds, and other investments. Knowing your income types is like understanding your car's gears – crucial for smooth financial driving.

But there's a wrinkle: gross income, the shiny number on your paycheck, isn't the whole story. Taxes, deductions, and various mouse-like entities take their cuts before you see your final share. That is net income, the true king of your financial castle. Learning this dance between gross and net is like cracking the tax code – you become the master, not the servant, of your money.

II. Understanding Income

The Income Ecosystem includes your active income, your salary, which is the steady stream powering your daily life. It's the money you earn from working your magic, whether it's coding pixels, crafting spreadsheets, or serving up lattes with a smile.

Passive income, on the other hand, is like planting a money tree – you put in the initial effort (investing, renting out a property), then reap the rewards over time, even while you sleep! Imagine waking up to rent checks or stock dividends – sweet financial sunshine, warming your bank account.

Then there's portfolio income, a hidden gem buried within investments like stocks and bonds. It's like owning a mini-business within your portfolio, earning dividends from company profits or interest from loans. It's a slower burn than active income, but like a slow-cooker, it creates long-term wealth with minimal daily effort.

Net vs. Gross: The Numbers Game

Think of gross income as a delicious birthday cake. It's tempting and impressive, but before you dig in, there's some slicing and dicing to do. Taxes, deductions for health insurance or retirement contributions, they're like the taxes your taste buds pay for the frosting. What's left after these deductions? That's your net income, the slice of the cake you actually get to enjoy.

Understanding this distinction is like learning to count calories – you become aware of how much "financial sugar" your paycheck carries and where it goes. This awareness is key to smart budgeting and mindful spending, empowering you to make conscious choices about your money.

Mastering the Income Landscape

Remember, income is just the first chapter in your financial odyssey. In the next chapters, we'll delve deeper into the art of taming your income:

- Expense Tracking: Unmasking the money monsters that gobble up your hard-earned loot.

- Savings Strategies: Building a financial fortress, brick by brick, for rainy days and future dreams.

- Tax Demystification: Navigating the tax code maze with confidence and maybe even a sprinkle of fun.

- Investment Alchemy: Transforming your savings into wealth-generating machines, making your money work for you.

With each chapter, your financial skills will sharpen, leading you toward a future where money is not a master, but a loyal companion on your life adventure.

Case Study: Memphis Oliver & Alex Noah: Navigating the Financial Jungle with Different Maps

Meet Memphis and Alex, two young adults embarking on their post-college journeys, but with vastly different financial compasses. Memphis, the social butterfly, landed a coveted marketing position at a trendy startup. Her salary is impressive, offering immediate gratification and a life filled with weekend brunches and spontaneous adventures. Alex, the creative soul, chose a freelance photography path, lured by the promise of flexibility and artistic freedom. His income fluctuates like the tides, sometimes overflowing, sometimes barely a trickle.

Income Streams:

Memphis enjoys the stability of active income, her regular monthly salary. Every payday, her bank account receives a predictable boost, allowing her to budget with confidence. Alex, on the other hand, navigates the unpredictable waters of passive income. His earnings depend on client projects, gigs, and occasional workshop fees. He experiences peaks and valleys, requiring adaptability and a strong financial buffer.

Spending Habits:

Memphis's consistent income fuels a carefree approach to spending. Dining out, weekend getaways, and trendy fashion trends are regular expenses. Saving feels like an afterthought, often overshadowed by the immediate allure of instant gratification. Alex, with his fluctuating income, has become a budgeting ninja. He tracks every penny, prioritizes needs over wants, and embraces frugality as a badge of honor. Every dollar saved is a victory against the unpredictable.

Investment Strategies:

Memphis's financial future feels distant, shrouded in the comfort of her current salary. Investing seems complex and unnecessary, pushed aside by the allure of immediate thrills. Alex, however, sees every lull in income as an opportunity to invest in himself. He takes free online courses, attends industry workshops, and builds his professional portfolio. His investments are intangible, but the returns are measured in skills, creativity, and long-term career growth.

Challenges and Triumphs:

Memphis's biggest challenge is delayed gratification. The temptation to live paycheck-to-paycheck is strong, leaving little room for financial security or future goals. Alex's struggle lies in the inconsistency. Months of feast can be followed by periods of famine, demanding resilience and resourcefulness.

However, both Memphis and Alex have their triumphs. Memphis, realizing the importance of saving, starts small, setting aside a portion of each paycheck into an emergency fund. Alex, through his calculated spending and continuous learning, lands a long-term contract with a prestigious magazine, stabilizing his income and validating his career choices.

Their stories highlight that there's no one-size-fits-all approach to money management. Memphis and Alex, with their contrasting income types, showcase that financial success is about adaptability, mindful spending, and a commitment to future goals. Regardless of whether your income is a steady stream or a gushing fountain, understanding your money habits, embracing smart financial strategies, and investing in yourself are the keys to navigating the financial jungle and building a life of security and happiness.

III. Expenses

You have conquered the income mountain; now it's time to face the expense dragon. These sneaky critters devour your loot, so understanding their habits is key to financial victory. We will dissect fixed expenses, those rent & utility monsters, and variable vampires like groceries and that extra latte (guilt-free in moderation, of course!).

Fixed Expenses: The Non-Negotiables

Think of these as the boss battles of your budget — they are unavoidable and often demand a significant chunk of your loot. Rent or mortgage payments, utilities (electricity, water, internet), insurance premiums, and subscription services (think gym memberships or streaming platforms) are common examples.

Variable Expenses: The Sneaky Shapeshifters

These expenses, which include groceries, transportation, entertainment, clothing, dining out, and other lifestyle choices, can be tamed with a bit of strategy.

Tracking Expenses: Your Financial X-Ray

Tracking your expenses is like deciphering the dragon's language. Every penny you spend, be it rent or ramen, gets logged in your expense tracker. It's like a financial X-ray, revealing spending patterns and hidden budget leaks. Think of it as an epic RPG quest – slaying bad spending habits and leveling up your financial wisdom.

Tools of the Trade:

- Pen and Paper: Go old-school with a trusty notebook and pen.

- Budgeting Apps: Embrace technology with apps like Mint, YNAB, or Personal Capital.

- Spreadsheets: Channel your inner Excel wizard and create custom trackers.

Tracking Tips:

- Log every penny: Be meticulous, track your expenses for a month – everything from rent to movie tickets, even if it's just a $2 coffee.

- Categorize expenses: Sort them into fixed (rent, utilities, subscriptions), variable (groceries, transportation, fun stuff), and debt repayments.

- Analyze your dragon's loot! Where does your money go? Are there unnecessary expenses you can slay? Can you optimize your fixed costs by negotiating bills or finding roommates? Review regularly: Set weekly or monthly check-ins to reflect on your spending patterns.

- Identify areas for improvement: Look for opportunities to cut back on unnecessary expenses or find more affordable alternatives.

Remember, this isn't about deprivation, it's about awareness. Once you know your financial landscape, you can make informed choices and allocate your loot wisely.

IV. Savings

Ah, saving – this is that magical small seed that grows into financial security. Whether it's a rainy day fund for unexpected car repairs or that dream vacation to Bali, every bit you save adds to your future forest. Don't underestimate the power of small, consistent savings – they snowball over time, compounding your financial might.

Planting Your Future Fortune. The 50/30/20 Rule: A Simple Blueprint for Success

- Needs
  (50%): Rent, groceries, utilities, transportation, health insurance.

- Wants (30%): Entertainment, dining out, shopping, hobbies, travel.

- Savings (20%): Emergency fund, retirement savings, debt repayment.

Automated Savings: Set It and Forget It

- Direct deposit: Automatically divert a portion of your paycheck to savings.

- Recurring transfers: Set up regular transfers from your checking to savings account.

- Round-ups: Apps like Acorns round up purchases to the nearest dollar and invest the spare change.

People who visualize their future goals (dream house, retirement bliss) saved more effectively. So, picture your financial oasis and let it fuel your saving fire!

- Imagine your dream home, a relaxing retirement, or a debt-free life.

- Create a visual reminder (vision board, wallpaper, or savings goal tracker) to keep your motivation high.

V. Taxes

Why We Pay Taxes: It's Not Just About the Gold

Taxes, the bane of every adventurer's existence, but understanding them unlocks hidden treasure! They are your contribution to building and maintaining roads, schools, and all the cool stuff society offers. Think of it as paying rent for the world we share.

- Funding essential public services like roads, schools, healthcare, and social programs.

- Contributing to a functioning society and a better quality of life for all.

Filing Taxes: A Quest with a Map

Filing taxes might seem like deciphering ancient scrolls, but fear not! W2s, tax deductions, and filing forms become friends once you learn their language.

- W2s: Forms from your employer detailing your income and taxes withheld.

- Tax deductions: Eligible expenses that reduce your taxable income (e.g., student loan interest, charitable contributions).

- Filing forms: Choose between 1040EZ, 1040A, or 1040 depending on your tax situation.

- Free filing options: The IRS offers free online filing for those with simple tax returns.

- Software and professional help: Tax software like TurboTax or H&R Block can guide you, or consult a tax professional for personalized advice.

VI. Investments

Now, let's talk about investments, the seeds you plant for long-term wealth. Stocks, bonds, and mutual funds are like magical beans that grow into financial trees. They help your money work for you while you sleep, generating passive income to fuel your future dreams.

Common Investment Types: A Stroll Through the Financial Forest

- Stocks: Ownership shares in companies, offering potential for growth and dividends.

- Bonds: Loans to companies or governments, providing fixed income payments.

- Mutual funds: Collections of stocks and bonds, offering diversification and professional management.

- Retirement accounts: Tax-advantaged accounts like 401(k)s and IRAs, designed for long-term savings.

Risk and Reward: The Balancing Act

Of course, investments come with risks – the financial wilderness has its share of storms. But, like Warren Buffett, the investing legend who started young, with patience and research, you can navigate the risks and reap the rewards. His story is a testament to the power of early and thoughtful investment.

- Higher potential returns often come with higher risks.

- Understand your risk tolerance and investment goals before making decisions.

- Research and consult with financial advisors to create a diversified investment portfolio that aligns with your goals.

VII. Conclusion

The Final Quest: Your Financial Future Awaits

Understanding money matters at an early age is like having a secret map to financial freedom. You've scaled income mountain, tamed the expense dragon, planted your saving seeds, befriended the tax beast, and learned the alchemy of investments. Now, the path to your financial future stretches before you, clear and bright. Remember, financial literacy isn't just about making money, it's about making informed choices and securing your future. Don't forget that!

Key Takeaways:

1. Tracking your expenses reveals hidden spending habits and empowers you to make informed choices.
2. Saving, even small amounts regularly, is crucial for building financial security and realizing future goals.

3. Taxes are an essential aspect of society, and understanding them helps you navigate the filing process smoothly.

4. Investments offer long-term financial growth but carry inherent risks. Research and consult experts.

Chapter 7

Budgeting 101 for Independent Living - Cracking the Code of Living Within Your Means

I. Introduction

Do you remember the thrill you got when you were launching into independent living? Turns out, freedom comes with one crucial companion: your budget. It's not a dusty old scroll with boring numbers, but your personal decoder ring for the financial jungle. This chapter, is your decoder key, cracking the code of living within your means and turning finances into a thrilling quest for financial security.

II. The Basics of Budgeting

Imagine a budget as your personal GPS or roadmap, helping you navigate the sometimes-tricky terrain of income and spending. Like I said before, it doesn't mean deprivation or strict rules, but about awareness and intentional choices. With this map, you dodge debt-filled potholes, fuel your dreams with strategic saving, reach your financial goals faster, and build a future where money works for you, not the other way around.

Benefits worth More Than Dragon's Hoard:

- Say NO to Debt: By understanding your limits, you become the knight slaying credit card vultures before they feast on your future income.

- Saving Sensei: Every penny becomes a stepping stone toward your dream vacation, a rainy-day shield, or that epic down payment on a life you design.

- Goal Getter: From a new phone to a dream house, financial goals, your personal

Everest, become achievable when you map your finances like an expert climber.

- Stress Slayer: Knowing where your money goes is like a soothing balm. It frees you from financial worry and lets you focus on the adventures that truly matter.

III. Creating and Maintaining a Personal Budget

Let's build your financial castle, brick by brick! Your first step is a thorough inventory:

1. Income Inventory:

Become a financial Indiana Jones (a legendary film character hero). Unearthing every source of income. First, calculate your monthly income from all sources. Include your salary, freelancing gigs, side hustles, and even birthday cash (Got to appreciate grandma's love!). Be meticulous, every occasional coin counts.

2. Expense Excavation:

Now, map your spending like a cartographer exploring uncharted territory. Categorize your expenses into two camps:

- Fixed Expenses: Rent, utilities, insurance – these essential outposts are the bedrock of your budget, non-negotiable but crucial for stability.

- Variable Expenses: Groceries, entertainment, that extra latte (a reward after conquering budget challenges, of course!). These can be adjusted and optimized to fit your financial landscape.

3. Goal Setting: Aim for the Financial Stars!

What makes your adventurous spirit sing? Is it a new camera for capturing epic moments, or is it a new phone, or a trip to Bali, to explore ancient ruins, or a career change to write your own life story? Define your short-term and long-term financial goals. These are your guiding stars, illuminating your budget priorities, like saving for that travel fund or allocating more toward skill development that fuels future income.

4. Building Your Budget Castle:

With your income, expenses, and goals mapped, it's time to construct your financial fortress! Here's your blueprint:

- Choose a method: Pen and paper, budgeting apps like Mint or YNAB, spreadsheets – pick your comfort zone.

- Allocate income: Assign chunks of your income to different categories based on your needs, wants, and goals. Prioritize essentials like rent and food, then factor in some fun (remember, balance is key!).

- Track your spending: Stay vigilant, adventurer! Regularly log your expenses to check if you're sticking to your plan.

- Adjust and adapt: Life throws curveballs. Be flexible and adjust your budget as needed. Maybe you cut back on dining out to invest in learning a new skill that boosts your future income.

Remember, your budget is not a rigid cage, but a flexible bridge. Embrace the journey, and watch your financial savviness soar!

IV. Real-Life Examples

Forget superheroes - real financial heroes walk among us! These inspiring young adults used budgeting to overcome challenges and achieve their financial goals:

1. The Backpacker: Emily from Seattle

Emily Chen, a 25-year-old barista with a wanderlust soul, dreamt of backpacking through Europe. Emily worked at "Bean & Brew," a popular local coffee shop in Seattle, but her monthly salary barely covered rent and groceries, let alone international travel. Undeterred, Emily embraced the power of a zero-based budget using the YNAB budgeting app to track her progress. She meticulously listed every expense, including rent, utilities, and even that daily latte, then allocated all of her income to specific categories. Every penny had a purpose.

She negotiated her internet bill, ditched cable for streaming services, and packed lunches instead of eating out. By sacrificing small luxuries, she freed up significant savings. She tracked her progress religiously, using a budgeting app to stay on track and celebrate milestones. Within a year, Emily had saved enough for a one-way ticket to Rome and a shoestring budget for her European adventure. She volunteered at a hostel in Barcelona to save on accommodation costs. Sleeping there, she learnt to cook simple but delicious meals on a budget, and utilizing free activities, she stretched her savings further, fulfilling her travel dreams without accumulating debt.

2. The Debt Crusader: David from Chicago

David Alvarez, a 27-year-old graphic designer, graduated from DePaul University with a degree in graphic design with a mountain of student loans of $40,000 in student loans from a combination of federal and private loans hovering over his head. The minimum payments felt like a treadmill he couldn't escape. Determined to break free, David tackled his debt with a snowball method. He listed his loans in order of smallest balance to largest, focusing on aggressively paying off the smallest one first. As each debt fell, he rolled the freed-up cash toward the next one, gaining momentum and motivation.

He also adopted side hustles like freelance graphic design projects and dog walking to boost his income. He took on extra freelance projects through websites like Upwork and Fiverr. Every extra dollar went toward his debt snowball, fueling his progress. This wasn't a quick fix - it took David two years of disciplined budgeting and hard work, but finally, he celebrated the last payment on his final loan. The experience transformed his financial mindset, equipping him with the knowledge and tools to manage his money proactively. Today, he now teaches a financial literacy workshop at his local community center.

3. The Homebuyer Heroes: Jessica and Michael from Austin

Jessica Hernandez and Michael Lee, both 30-year-old teachers teach science at Austin High School and yearned for their own home. But with rising housing costs and tight budgets, the dream seemed out of reach. They joined forces to create a shared budget, combining their incomes and streamlining their expenses. They researched their local housing market, setting a realistic budget based on their income and factoring in additional costs like property taxes and maintenance. They used a free online mortgage calculator to estimate their affordability range.

Instead of impulse purchases, they adopted a "needs vs. wants" approach, prioritizing rent, groceries, and bills. They tracked every expense, analyzed their spending patterns, and identified areas for improvement. They even negotiated their rent and secured a lower rate. Slowly, their savings account started to bulge.

With careful planning, budgeting, and sacrifice. They searched for a local realtor who specializes in first-time buyers and got a good deal for their money's worth. To help them power through, they hosted a fundraiser dinner with their friends and family to help with closing costs. Jessica and Michael saved enough for a down payment on a cozy starter home within two years and moved into their new home on their 3rd anniversary as a couple. Their story is a testament to the power of teamwork and disciplined budget management in achieving long-term financial goals.

These are just a few examples of real-life young adults who conquered their finances with different challenges and aspirations. Their stories are proof that success doesn't hinge on a high income but on dedication, resourcefulness, and a well-crafted budget.

Note, that every budget hero's journey is unique. Use their stories as inspiration, but tailor your budgeting strategy to your individual needs and goals. Embrace the tools and techniques in this chapter and embark on your own epic quest toward financial freedom!

Common Money Management Mistakes

How do you feel about that thrilling quest for independence? Navigating this new world requires a trusty map: your budget. Forget boring spreadsheets and dusty old rules. We're talking about a dynamic blueprint for financial freedom, customized to your epic goals and flexible enough to handle life's curveballs. This chapter, adventurer, is your decoder ring for cracking the code of living within your means.

We've all stumbled and fumbled in the money maze. But fear not! Recognizing these common traps early on can save you future headaches:

1. The Impulse Dragon: Swooping in with tempting one-click purchases and "limited-time" offers, this fiery beast can devour your budget. Breathe, adventurer! Before you unleash the "buy now" button, ask yourself: Do I need this? Can I get it cheaper elsewhere? Can I save for it instead? Taming the

Impulse Dragon requires mindful spending and prioritizing needs over fleeting desires.

2. The Debt Dungeon: Credit cards can seem like magical portals to instant gratification, but beware, adventurer! Their hidden fees and sky-high interest rates can trap you in a cycle of debt, draining your future wealth. Unless you're a Jedi Master of paying off balances in full every month, tread lightly in the Debt Dungeon.

3. The "FOMO" Fog: Seeing your friends splurge on fancy dinners and weekend getaways can trigger the dreaded Fear Of Missing Out. But remember, adventurer, everyone's journey is unique. Comparing your budget to someone else's highlight reel is like comparing apples to spaceships. Focus on your own financial goals and celebrate your milestones, big or small.

4. The Coffee Connoisseur Conundrum: That daily latte might seem harmless, but small pleasures can add up faster than you think. Track your spending closely and identify areas where you can cut back (hello, homemade cold brew!). Remember, small sacrifices today can fuel bigger adventures tomorrow.

V. Tips for Sticking to Your Budget

Building a budget is one thing, sticking to it is another. Here's your arsenal for keeping your financial fortress strong:

1. Track Your Every Treasure: Awareness is key, adventurer! Log your expenses daily, whether it's a movie ticket or a morning muffin. Use apps like Mint or YNAB, or a good old-fashioned notebook – whatever works for you. Seeing your spending habits laid bare is the first step toward making informed choices.

2. Review and Refine: Your budget isn't set in stone. Schedule regular check-ins (monthly, weekly, even daily if you're feeling adventurous) to analyze your spending and adjust your budget accordingly. Did that gym membership not spark joy? Cut it loose! Did your grocery expenses spike? Time to explore budget-friendly recipes.

3. Embrace Technology: The digital world is your financial playground! Budgeting apps like Mint, YNAB, or Personal Capital offer user-friendly interfaces, automated tracking, and even investment tips. Leverage the power of technology to simplify

your money management and free up time for epic quests of another kind.

4. Celebrate the Milestones: Every budget triumph deserves a victory dance! Did you reach your savings goal for that new gadget? Hit debt-free status? Treat yourself to a small reward (remember, mindful spending!). Celebrating your progress keeps you motivated and fuels your financial fire.

VI. Key Takeaways: Your Financial Compass

Before you embark on your independent living adventure, remember these guiding stars:

- Your budget is your roadmap to financial freedom. Treat it with respect and keep it updated to reach your destination.

- Awareness is your superpower. Track your spending and embrace technology to stay in control.

- Flexibility is key. Life throws curveballs, so adjust your budget when needed.

VII. Conclusion: The Journey Never Ends

Conquering your finances isn't a one-time event, adventurer. It's a continuous journey of learning, adapting, and growing. Keep an open mind, explore new financial tools and strategies, and most importantly, never stop asking questions. Remember, Claude AI is always here to guide you on your path to financial freedom.

VIII. Exercises & Activities:

- Build your own budget: Gather your income and expense statements and craft a personalized budget using any method that works for you.

- Track your spending for a week: Log every single expense, from that morning coffee to the movie ticket you bought on a whim. Analyze your spending patterns and identify areas for improvement.

- Challenge yourself: Set a small financial goal, like saving for a weekend getaway or paying off a credit card bill. Develop a plan.

Chapter 8:

Credit Score Decoded - Mastering the Magic Number

I. Introduction

The Cost of Swipes and Late Nights

Maya, a 27-year-old aspiring chef in Chicago, navigated the bustling city with a magnetic smile and a penchant for impromptu rooftop picnics and late-night jazz bars. Life was a whirlwind of flavor and spontaneity, fueled by credit cards and a "live now, pay later" mantra. Unfamiliar with credit scores, Maya saw credit lines as magical portals to endless possibilities, each swipe a culinary adventure in waiting.

The first warning bells arrived in the form of mounting statements and escalating minimum payments. The rooftop picnics started tasting a little bitter, the jazz notes echoing with anxiety. Every notification felt like a harsh reminder of her credit score - a dismal 520, the invisible scar of unchecked spending.

Dreams of opening her own fusion restaurant dimmed with each application. Landlords scrutinized her credit report, their initial warmth fading faster than Maya's hopes. Renting a decent apartment became a struggle, forcing her to share a cramped flat with fellow aspiring artists, the once independent chef reduced to a kitchen nomad in her own city.

The reality check came the day Maya received a dreaded call: her beloved motorcycle, the symbol of her freedom, was being repossessed. Watching it disappear through the cityscape, the weight of her choices hit her like a brick. The late-night swipes, the impulsive splurges, the unthinking spending - they had all converged into this suffocating reality.

The journey back was arduous. Maya devoured personal finance books, enrolled in online credit counseling courses, and meticulously crafted a budget, each line a brushstroke in her financial masterpiece. She negotiated her debts, juggled odd jobs, and learned the magic of budget-friendly meals (goodbye, takeout!). Every penny saved, every payment made on time, felt like a small victory, slowly chipping away at the mountain of debt and rebuilding her credit score.

It wasn't easy. There were early mornings fueled by black coffee instead of lattes, nights spent crunching numbers instead of catching jazz. But with each milestone, Maya saw a reflection of a different person: a responsible, determined chef taking control of her financial future. The carefree foodie had matured into a financial warrior, wielding her newfound knowledge and discipline like a trusty spatula.

The journey took a few years, but when Maya finally secured a loan to open her own fusion restaurant, the joy was tinged with the sweet taste of redemption. Her credit score, now a respectable 780, was a testament to her resilience and a badge of honor she wore with pride.

Maya's story is a cautionary tale, a reminder that financial freedom isn't an inherited right, but a hard-earned privilege. It's a story that resonates because it's not just about numbers; it's about dreams deferred, anxiety endured, and ultimately, the triumph of self-awareness and responsible action. In Maya, you see the importance of this chapter - not just as a theoretical exploration of credit scores, but as a practical guide to unlocking the door to a brighter financial future. Her journey is proof that the path to financial freedom, though paved with challenges, is ultimately one that any young adventurer can traverse, one step at a time.

II. Understanding Credit Score

The Credit Score Enigma: Numbers with Bite

Think of your credit score as your financial report card. It's a three-digit number ranging from 300 (Yikes!) to 850 (Financial Superhero!), calculated by credit bureaus like Experian, TransUnion, and Equifax. This magical number reflects your borrowing history, basically how responsible you've been with credit. Pay bills on time, keep debts low? Your score soars like a majestic eagle. Rack up late payments and carry high balances? You could be diving into shark-infested waters with a score plummeting faster than a dropped phone.

Unmasking the Credit Score Calculation

Here's how those three digits come to life:

- Payment History (35%): This is the big kahuna, adventurer. On-time payments are your best friends, boosting your score like a magic potion. Late payments, like trolls on your financial bridge, can send your score crashing down.

- Amounts Owed (30%): Don't be a debt dragon hoarder! Keeping your credit card balances low and not maxing them out shows responsible borrowing habits. Remember, less is more when it comes to debt.

- Length of Credit History (15%): Time is your ally, adventurer. The longer you've had credit accounts in good standing, the better. So, even that old student loan you're diligently paying is helping build your score!

- New Credit (10%): Avoid opening too many new accounts at once, it might raise eyebrows at the credit bureaus. Slow and steady wins the financial race!

- Types of Credit Used (10%): Having a healthy mix of credit, like a secured loan or a student loan, alongside your credit card, shows you can handle different types of borrowing responsibly. Diversity is key!

Your credit score is not a fixed sentence. It's a dynamic metric that responds to your financial choices. By understanding its secrets, avoiding common pitfalls, and managing debt wisely, you can transform this three-digit number from a nemesis to a loyal ally.

Why should you care, you ask?

A good credit score is your golden ticket to financial adulthood. It unlocks doors to better interest rates on loans, mortgages, even credit cards (remember, these can be tools, not traps!). With a stellar score, you snag the best deals, leaving more treasure for epic adventures, not debt repayments. Studies by The National Bureau of Economic Research show that a low credit score can cost you thousands in higher interest rates over your lifetime, basically forcing you to pay a premium for financial fumbles. Yikes!

III. Common Mistakes That Hurt Your Credit Score

The epic battle against debt! Even the bravest finance guru stumble, and when it comes to your credit score, certain mistakes can leave you vulnerable. Let's explore some common credit score kryptonite to avoid, and some spooky stats to keep you on your toes!

1. The Late Payment Plague: This is the ultimate credit score slayer. Missed deadlines are like rogue arrows piercing your financial armor, sending your score plummeting faster than a dropped phone. Remember Sarah from Chapter 1? One missed credit card payment snowballed into late fees and a score nosedive, reminding us: consistency is key!

Mark Coolio, a freelance photographer, prioritized his latest shoot over a credit card bill. That "little" oversight turned into a month-long delay, dropping his score by 60 points and making him ineligible for a low-interest loan he needed for new equipment. Lesson learned: set reminders, automate payments, and treat bills like fire-breathing dragons – handle them promptly!

2. The Debt Dragon Hoard: Maxing out credit cards or carrying high balances is like inviting debt dragons to take up permanent residence in your financial castle. Why? Credit utilization rate, the percentage of your credit limit you're using, plays a significant role in your score. Aim for a low utilization rate, ideally below 30%. Think of it as a financial tightrope walk – balance is key!

Emma Greene, a fashion blogger, loved online shopping sprees, forgetting the plastic sword she wielded had limits. Her maxed-out cards and ballooning balances sent her score spiraling down, making it tough to secure a loan for her dream boutique. Remember, adventurer, moderation is your magic shield – slay those debt dragons before they overwhelm you!

3. The Account Abandonment Myth: Closing old accounts in good standing might seem like a clean slate, but it can actually hurt your score! Why? Length

of credit history matters. The longer you've had accounts open and responsibly managed, the better. So, let those old accounts be your loyal financial companions, unless they're riddled with debt – then slay them with a vengeance!

John O'Brien, a recent college graduate, closed his old student loan after diligently paying it off. While he celebrated being debt-free, his score took a surprising dip. Closing the account, despite consistent payments, shortened his credit history, impacting his score. Remember, adventurer, age and wisdom (financial wisdom that is) are valued in the credit score kingdom!

Fact or Fiction? The Numbers Don't Lie: Research from Experian paints a sobering picture: nearly 30% of Americans struggle with poor or bad credit, often due to these very mistakes. Don't become a statistic, adventurer! With knowledge as your weapon and smart choices as your armor, you can conquer these credit score kryptonite monsters and build a fortress of financial stability.

IV. How to Improve Your Credit Score

Remember those pesky debt pitfalls we encountered previously? Well, fret not! This section is your guide to transforming them from fire-breathing threats into glittering treasure piles – by improving your credit score, that is. Think of it as financial alchemy, turning leaden debt into golden opportunities!

The Five Pillars of Score Sorcery:

1. The Punctuality Potion: Late payments are kryptonite to your score, adventurer. Slay them with the Punctuality Potion! Set automatic payments, calendar reminders, even tie a knot in your underwear if that helps – just ensure those bills get paid on time, every time. Consistency is your magic shield!

2. The Debt-Slaying Elixir: High balances are another dragon you don't want to cuddle. Keep your credit card balances low, ideally below 30% of your limit. Think of it as a financial tightrope walk – balance is key! Remember, moderation is your mantra – slay those debt dragons before they overwhelm you!

3. The Credit History Charm: Don't underestimate the power of age and wisdom,

even in the credit score realm. Keep those old accounts open and in good standing – they're like loyal companions boosting your score with their longevity. Unless they're riddled with debt, of course – then slay them with the Debt-Slaying Elixir!

4. The Credit Mix Mystery: Diversity is your friend, adventurer! Having a healthy mix of credit, like a car loan or a secured loan alongside your credit card, shows you can handle different types of borrowing responsibly. Experiment with different accounts, like potions in a wizard's lab, but always do so wisely!

5. The Credit Gremlins' Bane: Be vigilant, adventurer! Check your credit reports regularly for errors or discrepancies. Those sneaky Credit Gremlins can drag down your score with false information. Dispute them immediately, like a warrior confronting an unjust accusation!

Benefits of a Golden Score:

A stellar credit score isn't just a number to brag about, it's a key that unlocks a world of financial opportunity. Think of it as the ultimate treasure map:

- Lower Interest Rates: Say goodbye to loan shark rates, adventurer! With a good score, you'll snag the best deals on mortgages, car loans, and even credit cards, saving you thousands in the long run. Who says slaying dragons doesn't come with rewards?

- Higher Credit Limits: Forget scraping by with minimum limits. A good score unlocks doors to higher credit lines, giving you more financial flexibility and breathing room. Just remember, with great power comes great responsibility – wield it wisely!

- Better Rental Opportunities: Landlords love good credit scores, adventurer! Having one opens doors to nicer apartments, smoother renting processes, and maybe even that rooftop balcony you've been dreaming of. Who wouldn't want a dragon-slaying knight as a tenant?

A study by the Federal Reserve Bank of New York found that people with higher credit scores are 50% more likely to get approved for new credit than those with poor scores. Don't become a statistic! Embrace the Five Pillars of Score Sorcery and watch your credit score transform from leaden burden to golden opportunity!

V. Managing Debt Wisely

Let's delve into the different debt beasts you'll encounter and explore ways to manage them like a seasoned debt samurai.

The Debt Menagerie:

- Credit Card Chimera: This beast thrives on late payments and high balances. Slay it with the Punctuality Potion (automatic payments!) and Debt-Slaying Elixir (balance transfers and repayment plans!). Remember, moderation is key – don't let the Chimera turn your wallet into its lair!

- Student Loan Golem: This one might seem daunting, but it's often manageable with proper strategies. Explore income-driven repayment plans, loan consolidation options, and even career paths with loan forgiveness programs. Remember, knowledge is your weapon – research and consult financial advisors to outsmart the Golem!

- Medical Basilisk: This unexpected critter can emerge after unexpected medical bills. Negotiate payment plans, utilize medical assistance programs, and consider opening a medical credit card to manage the bites of the Basilisk. Remember, resilience is your shield – don't let its venom poison your financial well-being!

Taming Tales: Real-Life Debt-Slaying Adventures:

- Zara Foster, the Punctuality Queen: Sarah, once plagued by late payments, swore allegiance to the Punctuality Potion. By automating bills and setting calendar reminders, she slayed the Credit Card Chimera, boosting her score and securing a loan for her dream bakery. Remember, consistency is your crown – wear it with pride!

- David Kaplan, the Loan-Consolidation Master: David, burdened by multiple student loans, wielded the Loan Consolidation Elixir. He merged his loans into one with a lower interest rate, simplifying his repayments and saving thousands in the long run. Remember, strategy is your sword – use it to dissect your debt and devise the perfect plan!

- Maria Kutch, the Negotiation Ninja: Maria, facing unexpected medical bills, donned the Resilience Cloak. She negotiated payment plans with hospitals, utilized medical assistance programs, and even managed to snag a 0% APR medical credit card. Remember, resourcefulness is your armor – wear it boldly and face the Medical Basilisk!

VI. Conclusion

Remember, adventurer, managing debt is not a sprint, it's a marathon. With discipline, proper planning, and the tools you've acquired in this chapter, you can transform your financial landscape from a dragon-infested wilderness into a thriving kingdom of prosperity.

VII. Key Takeaways for Your Financial Quest:

- Your credit score is your financial report card, reflecting your borrowing history. Treat it with respect!

- Common mistakes like late payments and high balances can hurt your score. Avoid them like plague-ridden goblins!

- Tips like paying bills on time, keeping low balances, and diversifying your credit mix can help you slay the debt dragons and improve your score.

- Different types of debt require different strategies. Be a debt samurai, adapting your tactics to each beast!

- Managing debt and improving your financial situation is possible with dedication and smart choices. You hold the reins, adventurer – ride toward financial freedom!

Remember, knowledge is your compass, discipline is your steed, and financial planning is your map. With these tools in your arsenal, you can navigate the complexities of debt and emerge victorious, one step at a time. The path to financial freedom might be riddled with challenges, but remember, adventurer, you have the power to conquer them all!

Chapter 9

Student Loans and Scholarships: Navigating Education Financing Options
I. Introduction

Higher education equips us for career success but steep tuition often necessitates loans burdening graduates for years. Let's demystify these financing options - federal versus private loans, the impact of interest rates on repayment, considerations around borrowing prudently. We'll also explore leveraging free aid like abundant merit and need-based scholarships to keep debt manageable. This chapter is your personal decoder ring, helping you understand the two big players in this arena: student loans and scholarships. With informed planning, you can have an achievable path without unnecessary financial stress.

II. Section One: Understanding Student Loans

Loans fund school when savings fall short but should be a last resort after exhausting grants, work-study wages and scholarships. Federal loans come directly from government while private loans involve third-party lenders. Compare terms like origination fees and percentage rates annually compounding. Borrow only essential, conservative principal you can realistically repay in a decade. Excess debt becomes crushing.

Let's be honest, college is an investment in your future, and every investment needs a plan. Understanding financing options allows you to make informed decisions, avoid unnecessary stress, and graduate with a diploma AND a clear financial headspace. Plus, knowledge is power, and knowing your loan terms or scholarship requirements empowers you to navigate the system like a boss.

Student loans are basically money you borrow to pay for college, with the promise to repay it later (plus interest). Think of them as a temporary boost to reach your academic goals. There are two main types:

- Federal Loans: These come from the government and usually have lower interest rates and more flexible repayment options. Think of them as your supportive, understanding loan-shark (weird comparison, but roll with it).

- Private Loans: These come from banks or other lenders and often have higher interest rates and stricter terms. Think of them as the cool loan-shark with a leather jacket and questionable tattoos – proceed with caution!

Loan Pros and Cons:

Loans can be lifesavers, offering access to educational opportunities you might not otherwise have. They can also be burdens, so consider both sides:

Pros:

- Accessibility: They bridge the gap between your means and your educational dreams.

- Flexible repayment: Some repayment plans adjust based on your income, offering breathing room.

- Building credit: Responsible loan management can actually help build your credit score.

Cons:

- Debt, debt, and more debt: Graduation means not just a diploma, but potentially years of loan repayments.

- Interest adds up: Those sneaky percentages can significantly increase your overall repayment amount.

Stress factor: Looming debt can feel heavy and impact your future financial decisions.

For example, Mariah Cusack took out $68,000 in federal undergraduate loans between 2018-2022 to attend UCLA, accruing at an average of 6% interest compounded annually. Her minimum monthly payment over a 20-year standard repayment plan equals around $560. By the time Mariah's loans are forgiven after 240 months, she will have paid $134,400 total - over $66,000 of that interest alone.

In contrast, James Castro took $24,000 in loans to attend a local state college from 2019-2023, also with a 4% federal interest rate. Given his lower principal balance, James' minimum payment is just $170 monthly over a 6-year term before the debt is cleared. His total repayment adds up to $30,120, with interest accounting for $6,120 of extra costs due to borrowing.

This last scenario is the one I found most interesting; it's about Mercy Cole, a college graduate who tackled her student loans head-on. She researched repayment options, found an income-driven plan that fit her budget, and aggressively paid off high-interest loans first. With careful planning and dedication, she graduated debt-free and started her career without financial baggage. See? Loans can be navigated wisely!

III. Section Two: Managing Loans Wisely

Once borrowed, diligently maintaining payments prevents delinquency consequences like wrecked credit, garnished wages, seized tax refunds. Research flexible options like income-driven plans capping amounts due based on sustainable percentages of salary. Consolidation and refinancing may also ease strains for responsible graduates earnestly repaying despite adversity.

In summary, here's how to manage loans:

- Stay on top of payments: Missing payments hurts your credit and adds late fees. Set up automatic payments or reminders.

- Explore repayment options: Talk to your loan servicer about income-driven plans or consolidation options.

- Consider refinancing: If interest rates drop, see if refinancing to a lower rate can save you money.

- Live within your means: Avoid lifestyle inflation to make loan payments more manageable.

IV. Section Three: Understanding Scholarships

Scholarships are basically free money awarded based on merit, need, or specific criteria. Think of them as fairy godmothers waving financial magic wands (minus the pumpkin carriage). They come in various flavors:

- Academic scholarships: Awarded based on your GPA, test scores, or academic achievements.

- Need-based scholarships: Awarded to students with financial need.

- Athletic scholarships: Awarded to talented athletes.

- Minority scholarships: Awarded to students from specific ethnic or cultural backgrounds.

- Specific program scholarships: Awarded to students pursuing specific fields of study.

Benefits of Scholarship over Loans

Scholarships are awesome because they reduce your reliance on loans and free up future earnings for other goals. Here's why they are the better option:

- Free money, no strings (usually): You don't pay it back! (Read scholarship terms carefully to understand any obligations).

- Less debt, more freedom: Less reliance on loans means less financial stress and more financial flexibility.

- Can help create avenue for early career path, like students in sports or specific specialized fields of study.

- Open doors to opportunities: Some scholarships can cover not just tuition but also living expenses, opening doors to dream schools you might not have considered

V. Section Four: How to Find and Apply for Scholarships

Scholarships provide free aid but require proactive efforts assessing eligibility for the abundance available. Finding scholarships is like treasure hunting – you need the right tools and a dash of strategy. Here's your map to financial aid gold:

1. Search Engines: Online databases like Fastweb, ScholarshipOwl, and Unigo are your first stop. Filter

by your interests, GPA, background, and desired field of study. Remember, the more specific you are, the more relevant results you'll get.

2. College & University Resources: Every college has its own scholarship offerings. Explore their financial aid websites, talk to their scholarship advisors, and attend scholarship info sessions. They often have hidden gems exclusive to their students.

3. Local Communities: Don't overlook your own backyard! Check with high schools, community organizations, local businesses, and religious groups. They might offer scholarships based on community service, specific talents, or even financial need.

4. Professional Associations & Foundations: Industry-specific groups and foundations often offer scholarships in their fields. Explore their websites or contact them directly. This shows initiative and passion for your career path.

5. Niche & Unique Awards: Get creative! Look for scholarships based on unusual talents, hobbies, or even your heritage. There's a scholarship out there for almost everything, you just have to dig a little deeper.

Note that, this also works: Securing numerous smaller awards can add up significantly compared to a single elusive full-ride situation.

Conquering scholarship applications requires preparation and attention to detail. Here's your battle plan:

- Read instructions carefully: Each scholarship has specific requirements and deadlines. Follow them strictly – even minor mistakes can disqualify you.

- Strong essays: Craft compelling essays that highlight your achievements, goals, and unique qualities. Be genuine, specific, and showcase your passion for your chosen field.

- Letters of recommendation: Request them from teachers, mentors, or employers who can attest to your strengths and potential. Choose individuals who know you well and can write compelling testimonials.

- Transcripts & Standardized Test Scores: Make sure these documents are accurate and submitted on time.

Alexandra Goldberg, a driven student who just finished her marine biology degree in 2022 having secured over $38,000 in scholarships by her graduation day at the University of Miami. Rather than feel overwhelmed by the costs of higher education, Alexandra made unlocking financial aid opportunities a priority early on.

During her junior year of high school back in 2018, she began actively seeking potential awards in her anticipated field of ocean conservation research. Alexandra tailored each application to emphasize her academic achievements, voluntary reef clean-up initiatives she founded locally, and profound passion for the oceans evidenced by a 500-word personal statement on threats of erosion compelling judges with vivid urgency.

Beyond generalized databases, she utilized niche marine science scholarship engines to target funding earmarked for women pursuing STEM degrees. Alexandra also impressed the faculty at Rosenstiel School of Marine Science with her initiative cold emailing every professor in the department to advocate her candidacy for their undergraduate endowments. Through determined efforts submitting countless applications over years aligned strategically with her goals, Alexandra secured over 25 smaller renewable scholarships averaging $1,500 yearly. This diligence allowed her to emerge debt-free and fully equipped to take on her dream environmental role protecting fragile coral ecosystems.

VI. Section Five: Balancing Between Student Loans & Scholarships

Loans and scholarships are like yin and yang in education financing. Let's learn how to find the perfect balance:

1. Assess Your Needs: Before diving in, honestly evaluate your financial situation. How much can your family contribute? What are your estimated living expenses? This helps you determine how much financial aid you truly need.

2. Prioritize Scholarships: Maximize free money first! Seek scholarships aggressively and apply early. Every dollar you earn through scholarships translates to less loan debt later.

3. Use Loans Wisely: If loans are necessary, choose federal options with lower interest rates and flexible

repayment plans. Remember, loans are an investment, not free money. Borrow only what you truly need and can afford to repay.

4. Track Your Finances: Create a budget and track your income and expenses carefully. This helps you stay on top of your finances and manage loan repayments effectively.

5. Consider Work-Study Options: Federal work-study programs allow you to earn money while in school. This can help reduce your reliance on loans and provide valuable work experience.

Remember: There's no one-size-fits-all answer. The right balance between loans and scholarships depends on your unique circumstances. Seek professional financial aid and guidance if needed.

VII. Conclusion:

By taking control of your education financing, you're investing in your future success. Remember:

- Knowledge is power: The more you understand your options, the better equipped you are to make informed decisions.

- Start early: Don't wait until the last minute to research financing options. Early planning allows for strategic exploration and scholarship applications.

- Be proactive: Don't wait for opportunities to come to you. Actively research scholarships, network, and make informed choices.

- Financial literacy is freedom: Taking control of your finances now empowers you to achieve your goals without the burden of debt.

Navigating education financing can be tricky, but remember, you're in control! In summary, this chapter provided tools and strategies to:

- Understand loan and scholarship options

- Find and apply for scholarships effectively

- Balance loans and scholarships wisely

Take Action, Own Your Future:

- Start researching financing options early, even before applying to colleges.

- Talk to financial aid advisors at your chosen schools and explore their unique scholarships.

- Don't be afraid to ask for help! Financial aid professionals are there to guide you.

- Remember, responsible financial decisions now pave the way for a brighter, debt-free future.

VIII. Key Takeaways:

- Know your financial needs before borrowing.

- Explore all scholarships options before taking out loans.

- Manage student loans wisely to avoid debt traps.

- Don't be passive: actively seek scholarships.

- Financial literacy is empowering: take control of your education financing!

Part III:

Getting Along with Others in the Adult World

Chapter 10

Communication Essentials: Articulate Your Thoughts Effectively

I. Introduction

Communication skills like active listening and verbal clarity are crucial for success personally and professionally, enabling better relationships and outcomes. Imagine landing your dream job, nailing that presentation, or charming your way into an epic adventure. Guess what's the secret sauce? Effective communication! Don't believe it? Harvard says 85% of your workplace success relies on soft skills, and communication rules that roost. Ready to unlock your inner communication skill?

II. Section One: Understanding Communication

Communication has many forms - verbal, nonverbal, written. It involves encoding messages sent to a receiver who interprets meaning and provides feedback, all impacted by noise. Clear expression considers this entire cycle.

Think of communication as the magic bridge connecting you to the world. You say something (verbal), hint with your body (non-verbal), or write it down (written), and voila! Your message travels. Isn't that fantastic? But it's a two-way street. This magic bridge has a "sender" (you), a "receiver" (the awesome person you're talking to), and "feedback" (their response). Imagine sending a joke across the bridge and getting crickets back – not ideal. Effective communication ensures your message lands like a high-five, not a faceplant.

III. Section Two: The Art of Listening

Hold up, communication isn't just about talking. Listening is equally important, maybe even more! Picture two college friends, Anjali and Ezequiel, who grab coffee at their usual campus spot one stressful finals week.

Anjali vents about barely sleeping while struggling to finish a big group project. But Ezequiel distracted by text messages on his phone, just nods vaguely during her sharing, not absorbing the importance of what she says. Later, when Anjali tries to follow up with Ezequiel about the project, she feels hurt realizing he didn't fully listen or understand her frustration that day. Ouch!

This disconnect highlights why active listening matters - it's not just waiting for your turn to talk. It means facing the speaker, paying attention to their words and asking clarifying questions to confirm understanding. An engaged listener also watches for nonverbal cues - are they tense or upset? Research by Wright State University in 2017 found active listening skills predicted the building of stronger relationships - and who doesn't want deeper bonds with loved ones?

So next time a friend is sharing resist the urge to multitask. Truly focus on their message without distractions. Show you care through thoughtful responses. You may discover communication is a two-way street requiring listening first, to understand then be understood.

Attentive listening facilitates mutual understanding between speaker and listener by allowing thoughtful decoding and response. Failures to listen actively can worsen conflicts or dissolve bonds. Studies show active listening builds better relationships.

IV. Section Three: Mastering Verbal Communication

So, you've listened well, now it's your turn to speak. Verbal communication is your chance to express yourself clearly and captivatingly. Think of it as crafting a message that sticks. Here are some spells to cast:

- Clarity: Ditch the jargon and mumbling. Use simple, powerful words that paint a picture in the listener's mind.

- Brevity: Time is precious, so get to the point. No one enjoys listening to someone ramble for hours.

- Positivity: Focus on the solution, not the problem. People gravitate toward upbeat communicators.

Remember, words have power. A study by the University of California, Berkeley, found that positive language can actually boost your persuasive power. Pretty cool, huh?

Verbal communication transmits information vocally, requiring attention to factors like word choice, brevity and tone for reception of intent. Examples where strong verbal skills produced favorable results.

V. Section Four: Communicating Nonverbally

We all know actions speak louder than words, and in communication, that's especially true. Non-verbal cues like body language, facial expressions, and even your tone of voice can convey volumes. Research from UCLA suggests that a whopping 93% of communication effectiveness comes from non-verbal cues! So, what are you saying without saying anything?

- Body Language: Stand tall, make eye contact, and avoid fidgeting. These project confidence and openness.

- Facial Expressions: A genuine smile goes a long way. Avoid scowling or looking bored – it sends the wrong message.

- Tone of Voice: Don't sound monotone! Vary your pitch and pace to keep things interesting.

Practice makes perfect, so experiment and find your sweet spot. Remember, effective communication is a journey, not a destination. So, get out there, practice your skills, and watch your world open up!

Nonverbal signals like facial cues and body language reinforce or undermine messages, conveying up to 93% of understanding by some accounts. Sensitivity to nonverbal hints aids expression.

VI. Section Five: Written Communication

Remember that magic bridge from before? Well, get ready to expand it further because written communication is crucial in today's digital age. From nailing college applications to acing online interviews, mastering the written word unlocks a whole new level of connection.

Emails, texts and messaging, social media posts carry growing influence– they're all your written voice and necessitating care-conveying-tone and clarity in writing. Tactics like previewing purpose, thoughtful editing, tailored formality levels based on audience and focused brevity boost reception. Whether you're applying for a job or catching up with friends, clear and concise writing makes a powerful impression. Here's your writing toolkit:

- Clarity is King: Imagine someone's reading your message on a tiny phone screen. Use short sentences, avoid jargon, and proofread like a hawk. Nobody likes deciphering cryptic messages!

- Structure Matters: Organize your thoughts. Start with a clear introduction, state your point, and end with a call to action. Think of it like building a strong bridge – clear sections guide your reader smoothly.

- Tone it Right: Whether it's a formal email or a casual text, adjust your tone accordingly. Remember, even online, respect goes a long way.

Need an example? Imagine asking your friend to join you for coffee. Instead of "hey sup u wanna hang?" ('shudder,' because it's unclear what you mean), try "Hey [Friend's Name]! Would you be interested in grabbing coffee sometime next week?" See the difference? It's all about being clear, friendly, and professional. However, it depends on the level of familiarity between you. Some unusual words could be an informal communication code among buddies.

VII. Section Six: Overcoming Communication Barriers

Communication isn't always smooth sailing. Language differences, cultural backgrounds, even personality clashes can create walls. But fear not, communication ninja! Stanford University research shows that by being mindful of these barriers, you can build bridges instead:

- Language Differences: Speak slowly and clearly, avoid slang, and be patient. Online translation tools can help, but remember, they're not perfect.

- Cultural Understanding: Research cultural norms and avoid making assumptions. A simple "Excuse me, can you clarify what you mean by that?" can go a long way.

- Respectful Communication: Be mindful of tone, humor, and body language. What's funny in one culture might be offensive in another.

Remember, effective communication is about connection, not winning arguments. Be open-minded, respectful, and willing to learn – these are the tools for building bridges across any boundary.

Language differences, cultural norms and conflicting styles of directness create communication gaps solved through patience, active listening clarification and mutual adjustment. Research from Stanford identifies openness as key.

VIII. Conclusion

Communication involves articulating thoughts verbally and nonverbally with active listening at its core. Mastering expression and reception dynamics enables deeper relationships and outcomes.

By this point, you've unlocked the secrets of verbal, non-verbal, and written communication. You've learned the importance of active listening and how to overcome different barriers. But remember, communication is a lifelong journey. Practice makes perfect, so don't be afraid to experiment, make mistakes, and learn from them.

IX. Your Call to Action:

Step out there and use your newfound communication skills! Talk to new people, express yourself confidently, and write like a pro. Soon, you'll be building bridges, opening doors, and conquering the world, one conversation at a time. Remember, effective communication is your superpower – use it wisely!

X. Key Takeaways:

- Communication comes in many forms: verbal, non-verbal, and written.

- Active listening is crucial for understanding others.

- Clear, concise communication is key in all forms, whether spoken or written.

- Be mindful of cultural and language differences to avoid misunderstandings.

- Practice makes perfect – the more you communicate, the better you'll become.

Remember, effective communication is not just about getting your point across, it's about connecting with others and building meaningful relationships. So go forth, young communicator, and conquer the world!

Chapter 11

Interpersonal Skills – Building Healthy Relationships

I. Introduction

Building strong relationships takes effort, but it is effort that pays lifelong dividends. Whether in your personal or professional life, the ability to connect with others creates bonds that provide meaning, support, enrichment, and opportunities. This chapter provides insights and strategies to help you build the skills needed to develop healthy, lasting relationships.

II. Understanding Interpersonal Skills

Interpersonal skills refer to your ability to effectively interact with others. These include communication skills like clear speaking and active listening as well as emotional skills like empathy, understanding nonverbal cues, managing conflict, and providing support. Researchers have shown interpersonal skills are vital for personal well-being and success at work and school (Kothari, et al., 2014). People who master interpersonal skills tend to have more friends, higher self-esteem, better relationships, and advanced careers.

There are many specific interpersonal skills that allow you to initiate, build, and maintain strong connections. Key skills include:

Communication - Clearly conveying thoughts, feelings, ideas, and information through speaking and writing. Using communication tools like humor and storytelling.

Empathy - Understanding others' perspectives, being able to put yourself in someone else's shoes.

Emotional intelligence - Recognizing and managing your emotions and reactions. Understanding how your words/actions impact others.

Active listening - Paying full attention, avoiding interruptions and distractions. Reflecting back what you hear others say.

Resolving conflict - Addressing disagreements with patience and respect. Finding solutions that meet both parties' needs.

III. The Role of Communication in Relationships

Out of the many interpersonal skills, communication serves a foundational role in building robust relationships. Poor communication leads to the bulk of conflicts within friendships, families, and romantic partnerships. Without clear communication, resentment and misunderstandings arise.

For example, imagine a situation where your partner fails to come home one evening and doesn't answer their phone. You may feel anger or worry. But perhaps they sent a text explaining they needed to work late and couldn't access their phone. With some simple communication, frustration could have been averted. It's easy to see how small breakdowns in conveying critical information can put relationships at risk when they accumulate over time.

True communication goes beyond just exchanging facts and information - it also entails sharing desires and emotions in a constructive way. Discussing hopes, fears, and vulnerabilities allows for deeper bonds. For instance, telling a friend "I felt concerned when I didn't hear from you all weekend" opens an honest conversation about needs in the relationship.

Some ways you can improve communication skills include:

- Practicing active listening skills when others speak

- Expressing your own needs and feelings clearly

- Giving constructive feedback, not just criticism

- Avoiding assumptions about others' motivations

- Writing a letter to explain complex thoughts and emotions

Keep in mind communication is always a work in progress. There will be occasional misunderstandings, lowered signals, and steps backwards. What matters most is the overall trajectory toward more open, supportive, and sincere communication.

IV. Empathy - Understanding Others' Perspectives

Empathy involves seeing a situation from another person's perspective, and imagining what thoughts, motivations, and feelings they may be experiencing. Researchers have found empathy facilitates social competence and behaviors that benefit relationships (Preston & de Waal, 2002). Demonstrating empathy forges an emotional bridge between you and others in your social circle.

For example, showing empathy could sound like: "I appreciate you must be feeling overwhelmed with your mom being sick and all your added responsibilities". Or, "I can imagine how exhausting it must be to work night shifts and deal with rude customers all day".

Empathy demonstrates emotional intelligence because it reveals an understanding of friends' and loved ones' internal states. It also signifies compassion for their hardships - that you "get" them on a deeper level. The other person then feels respected, valued, and less alone in their suffering.

Ways you can cultivate more empathy and perspective-taking include:

- Observing others' facial expressions and body language for emotional cues

- Listening without interruption when someone is sharing problems

- Avoiding trying to "one-up" others when they share difficulties

- Reading articles and books featuring people different than yourself

- Volunteering with marginalized groups to expand your understanding

Keep in mind empathy does not necessarily mean agreeing with another's actions or perspectives. However, leading with empathy provides a framework of respect for connecting even amidst disagreements.

V. Active Listening - Paying Attention to Others

You may think listening comes naturally, but going beyond passive listening to engaged, active listening requires both skill and effort. Unlike hearing others, active listening involves giving your full concentration, avoiding distractions, and demonstrating through body language and verbal affirmations that you grasp the messages being communicated (Bodie, et al., 2015).

For example, nodding your head, making eye contact, and interjecting occasionally demonstrates mental focus and confirms you are tracking what the other person says. Restating or summarizing key points also exhibits comprehension while clarifying any misheard statements.

Research on active listening shows it facilitates:

- Mutual understanding between conversation partners

- Perceptions of being "heard" and cared for

- Resolution of cross-cultural or interpersonal conflicts

- Higher rates of disclosure and intimacy

Active listening not only builds bonds in the moment, it also creates longer-lasting feelings of being understood and connected within relationships.

Some tips for honing your active listening skills include:

- Avoiding interrupting others before they finish speaking

- Focusing your attention without getting distracted

- Asking clarifying questions or rephrasing key points

- Expressing verbal affirmations like "yes" and "uh huh"

- Facing the speaker and making eye contact

Keep in mind active listening does not necessarily mean you agree with the speaker. However, it does communicate respect and care. Even amid disagreement, attentive listening provides the basis for mutual understanding.

The skills presented in this chapter require dedication and practice to master. However, emphasizing communication, empathy, and sincere listening in your interactions positions you to nurture healthier, more supportive relationships that stand the test of time. With some consistent effort, you will find these practices gradually shaping you into a caring, understanding friend and confidant.

VI. Conflict Resolution – Navigating Disagreements Healthily

It's inevitable you'll periodically experience conflict in your interpersonal relationships - disagreements are a natural part of social dynamics and interactions. How you respond in those heated moments impacts whether the conflict brings you closer together or slowly erodes the relationship. Researchers have identified various conflict resolution styles people use, with some being far more beneficial than others (Kurdek, 1994).

Destructive approaches involve expressing anger aggressively without concern for the other party, giving threats/ultimatums, stubbornly avoiding discussion, or pretending no conflict exists in the first place. These tactics typically fail to resolve disagreements and often make problems worse long-term by fostering resentment and emotional distance.

In contrast, constructive conflict resolution requires:

- Staying even-tempered, avoiding emotional outbursts
- Being respectful even when disagreeing
- Finding areas of common understanding
- Compromising to meet both parties' core needs
- Forgiving past hurts and letting go of grudges

These methods do not mean totally appeasing others or abandoning your own legitimate needs. Rather constructive conflict resolution provides a framework of listening, care, and respect so creative solutions can emerge - allowing for disagreement without division or ill-will.

Here are some pro tips for resolving conflicts in a growth-oriented way:

- Take a 24-hour break if emotions are running high before reengaging
- Use "I feel" statements instead of blaming others
- Seek areas where you can validate the other's perspective
- Identify solutions where both parties' core needs are met

With practice, you can make huge strides in managing disagreements and nurturing understanding - bringing people closer rather than pushing them apart.

VII. Building and Maintaining Relationships

While establishing connections comes fairly naturally early on, effort is required to sustain healthy relationships for the long haul. Researchers have identified key maintenance behaviors that counteract the inexorable forces pulling friends and partners apart over time (Rusbult & Van Lange, 2003). These include:

- Regularly expressing appreciation, affection, validation

- Sharing enjoyable experiences and making new memories

- Self-disclosing personal details to deepen intimacy

- Providing emotional and instrumental support

- Using inclusive language like "we" and "us"

Make no mistake, failing to adequately invest in relationship maintenance leads to disengagement, negativity, and dissolution regardless of previous closeness. Life's chaos and changing circumstances relentlessly conspire against human bonds if they are not consciously nurtured.

On the other hand, dedicating yourself to consistent relationship care yields great dividends for all parties:

- Enhanced self-esteem and life satisfaction

- Greater sense of belonging and support

- Deepened mutual understanding and intimacy

- Improved collaboration toward shared goals

The key is integrating maintenance behaviors into your routine interactions rather than leaving nourishment of your connections to chance. For example, sending a thoughtful text, bringing home flowers unexpectedly, or taking a friend out to that new brunch place integrates relational nourishment into regular life.

By actively investing in those you care about, you counteract natural decaying forces. And you build bonds that provide support, companionship, and meaning for years to come.

VIII. Conclusion:

Whether at home, at work, or in the community - your well-being is intimately intertwined with the quality of your relationships. The interpersonal skills presented in this chapter, including communication, empathy, listening, and conflict resolution, provide a roadmap to nurturing the healthy connections that support and enrich your life.

While building strong relationships requires effort, it repays that effort many times over. People who consistently nurture their social connections reap tangible benefits including greater confidence, support during difficult times, collaborators toward shared goals, and a heightened sense of belonging.

The strategies outlined here offer guideposts as you cultivate your ability to relate with others. Stay committed to growth. Though there may be missteps along the way, your dedication will bear fruit in the form of robust bonds that weather life's ups and downs.

Key Takeaways:

1. Interpersonal skills are crucial for building healthy relationships.

2. Effective communication, empathy, active listening, conflict resolution are key components of interpersonal skills.

3. Regularly practicing these skills can significantly improve your personal and professional relationships.

Additional Resources:

- Crucial Conversations by Patterson, Grenny, McMillan, & Switzler

- Nonviolent Communication by Marshall Rosenberg

- Getting Together and Staying Together by William Glasser

- Wired for Dating by Stan Tatkin

The journey awaits. Here's to meaningful connections!

Chapter 12

Conflict Resolution Strategies: Dealing With Disagreements Effectively

I. Introduction

We all face conflicts in our lives. Learning constructive ways to navigate disagreements and communicate through differences empowers us to build stronger relationships and achieve personal growth. As the saying goes – a smooth sea never made a skilled sailor. This chapter provides perspectives and techniques for facing conflicts head-on, understanding different viewpoints, and resolving tensions effectively.

II. Understanding Conflict

Conflict arises whenever incompatible needs, interests, values, or beliefs create tension between people, groups, or even within one's self. While the word "conflict" evokes notions of hostility and antagonism, it can manifest in relatively benign ways. For example, preferring different movies to watch or where to vacation introduces conflict in choosing which need or want takes priority. More deeply rooted tensions may stem from clashing communication styles, cultural norms, political divisions, or core psychological needs going unmet between parties.

Why does conflict occur at all? Various factors can ignite tensions:

- Basic human needs going unfulfilled – Conflict often signals core requirements specified in Maslow's hierarchy are being thwarted within a relationship. For instance, if respect, trust, or affection deteriorates, rifts are likely to emerge.

- Differing priorities + constraints – With limited resources like time and money, trade-offs spur disagreements, especially if priorities differ between groups or individuals.

- Perceived incompatibility – Conflict does not require actual incompatible goals, just the belief goals are opposing. For example, managers may perceive employees as threatening profitability, while employees perceive management as diminishing quality of life. Each group believes the other obstructing their interests.

While friction can fuel resentment between parties, conflict itself is not inherently negative or destructive. Handled constructively, disagreements produce improved understanding, credibility, innovation, and relationships. However, without mindful resolution the costs multiply rapidly.

III. The Impact of Poor Conflict Management

Unresolved tensions risk accumulating past the point of potential benefits. Researchers have extensively documented the high toll of poorly managed conflict (De Dreu, 2008), including:

- Hardened negative perceptions between groups

- Toxic culture rife with criticism, blame, obstruction

- Alienation, anxiety, depression in individuals

- Goal/task abandonment

- Loss of creativity, experimentation, efficiency

As conflicts linger without resetting understanding, communication continues deteriorating. Once collegial partners can spiral into resentful enemies, feeling threatened rather than trusted. Psychological defenses erect barriers blocking cooperative reconciliation. Hostility replaces goodwill while problems fester and multiply.

Of course, avoiding or ignoring conflict fails to make it disappear – latent tensions still limit relationships and progress. The alternative path promises greatly expanded horizons.

IV. The Benefits of Effective Conflict Resolution

While disagreements inherently produce discomfort, skillfully working through that discomfort births tremendous potential. Resolving conflict successfully:

- Generates mutual understanding

- Stimulates critical thinking and creativity

- Identifies problems needing attention

- Increases intimacy and communication

- Gains commitment to durable solutions

- Boosts team cohesion and morale

- Reduces hostility and resentment

Rather than allowing periods of conflict to shadow relationships, conscious steps can renew bonds between individuals even stronger than before. This highlights principles for engaging disagreement effectively.

V. Principles for Effective Conflict Resolution

1. Active Listening: The foundation for working through disagreements constructively involves temporarily suspending your perspective to focus completely on understanding another

party's experience. This entails paying full attention without interruption, avoiding assumptions, and reflecting back what you hear (conflict resolution through active listening allows identifying solutions meeting everyone's core needs).

2. Expressing Feelings Appropriately: Sharing feelings candidly while owning them introspectively calms tension. Use "I feel X emotion when Y behavior/situation occurs" statements to convey your experience constructively without blaming others. Communicate any hurt, fear, uncertainty prompting your reactions honestly but respectfully.

3. Seeking Win-Win Solutions: Rather than framing conflicts as win/lose battles for supremacy, identify solutions allowing all sides' fundamental needs being met. This requires empathy, creativity and compromise guided by mutual understanding, not fixed positions. Generate possibilities, evaluate jointly and gain consent from all parties.

4. Respect Differences: Recognizing diverse communication styles, cultural norms and psychological needs inherent across humanity defuses tendencies to judge or demand conformity. Express genuine appreciation for alternate worldviews. Embrace disagreements as opportunities to expand understanding of truth's multidimensionality.

The skills of compassionate communication, emotionally intelligent framing of differences and creative compromise allow navigating conflict's inevitability while strengthening relationships. With practice, you can gain confidence engaging disagreements and diversity with finesse – deepening bonds, broadening perspectives and catalyzing progress.

While conflict provokes discomfort, handled with care it births understanding and possibility. Approach tensions proactively and principles introduced here will serve you well on the journey ahead.

VI. Step-by-Step Guide to Resolving Conflicts

When embroiled in a disagreement, referencing this conflict resolution process can help restore understanding:

1. Identify the Problem: Name the specific issue openly and honestly without blaming. Use neutral language parties can agree upon to establish a baseline. For example, rather than accusing someone of being inconsiderate, state objective facts – "I've noticed the kitchen hasn't been cleaned in two weeks."

2. Understand Interests: Probe beneath stated positions to uncover all sides' underlying needs, concerns and motivations driving reactions. Employ active listening and insightful questioning. Ask "Why is this issue important to you?" to elicit deeper clarity.

3. Brainstorm Solutions: Specify success criteria then rapidly generate a broad range of potential settlement options. Set a creative, noncritical tone. Every voice offers input including unconventional solutions. A roommate conflict over guest policies might generate ideas like: rotational standards, house

meetings discussing visits, an online calendar system, or noise monitors giving feedback.

4. Negotiate Agreement: Discuss pros/cons of leading proposals that may satisfy both parties' core interests. Seek win-win compromises addressing essential priorities with mutual sacrifice. Detail next action steps, metrics and responsibilities clearly so all feel accountable.

VII. Real Life Examples

Relationships often benefit when parties translate conflict resolution principles into action. For example:

Roommate chores dispute:
After months of arguments, roommates Emma and Nicole implemented a conflict resolution process. Emma explained her full-time internship made chore expectations unreasonable. Rather than accusing her of laziness, Nicole listened empathetically. Understanding each other's situations revealed a shared desire for household functionality and fairness. Brainstorming produced ideas like a rotating schedule based on hours worked, hiring cleaning help, or rewarding chores with small incentives.

Negotiating session resulted in trying a website app tracking duties and allowing customized rotations based on evolving availability.

Workplace project disagreement: Facing a tight product launch deadline, colleagues Sarah and David disagreed on a feature set. Sarah felt adding functionality answered customer requests but required delay. David prioritized timing given competitors also launching offerings. Rather than forcing opinions, both postponed initial reactions to ask genuine questions uncovering needs and constraints. The team then brainstormed integrative solutions, realizing they could retain most desired capabilities and launch on schedule by dropping nonessential features. Their negotiated agreement committed all team members while ensuring continued dialog as progress unfolded.

VIII. Common Conflict Resolution Mistakes

Attempting to resolve tensions without mindful strategy frequently backfires, including:

- Judging rather than listening openly
- Dodging needed conversations

- Forcing solutions without collaboration

- Compromising on non-essential priorities

- Failing to gain mutual commitment

These approaches often exacerbate disagreements and damage relationships due to lingering unaddressed issues.

For example, when roommates avoid discussing cleaning conflicts, resentment builds over time. Or workplace teams that move forward without addressing objections risk substandard results.

IX. Enhancing Conflict Resolution Skills

Growing your competencies in navigating disagreement involves:

- Practicing active, non-judgmental listening

- Expressing feelings through "I statements"

- Role-playing negotiations seeking mutual gains

- Journaling to self-reflect after conflicts

Build confidence addressing tensions positively over time through purposeful effort. Attend skill-building workshops and read books like "Crucial Conversations".

X. Conclusion

Conflict sparks discomfort but yields understanding and possibility. Equip yourself to traverse disagreements constructively using communication principles and processes presented here. Resolution opens the door to improved relationships and growth.

XI. Key Takeaways

1. Conflicts are normal but productive if handled collaboratively.

2. Listen actively, express feelings appropriately and seek win-win solutions.

3. Avoid common pitfalls like avoiding issues or forcing unilateral outcomes.

4. Intentional practice strengthens constructive conflict resolution skills.

The journey awaits. Here's to relationships strengthened through conflict engagement!

Chapter 13

Networking Skills: Building Valuable Relationships for Personal and Professional Growth

I. Introduction

Connecting with others creates opportunity. While networking often gets reduced to collecting business card collections or expanding social media follower counts, at its core lies the joy of human interaction and relationship building. This chapter provides perspectives and strategies for developing genuine connections that support both personal fulfillment and professional goals.

II. The Science Behind Networking

Scientific insights validate an ancient truth – people thrive through social bonds fostering cooperation and growth. In a landmark meta-analysis of over 300,000 participants, researchers found those engaging social relationships dramatically increased their likelihood of survival over isolated peers (Holt-Lunstad et al., 2010). Beyond just correlating with longer lifespans, researchers cite significant evidence of connections improving health, happiness, resilience, knowledge and innovation (Rath, 2006).

This "social advantage" emerges from both the emotional nurturance received from trusted confidants as well as information and collaboration benefits accessed through wider supportive communities. Of course, surface-level social links should not be confused for the profound mutual understanding and care defining deep human relationships. However, even looser ties within thoughtfully developed networks create value.

III. Understanding Your Network

Many overlapping networks organically arise as you travel through various life domains. Key networks include:

Personal Networks – Close friends and family members with whom you share vulnerabilities, intimacy and support during adversity.

Professional Networks – Trusted contacts made through education, jobs, conferences etc. that enable career opportunities through information sharing and visibility of your expertise to those in your field.

Community Networks - Civic, religious, hobbyist groups creating belonging, knowledge and the power to catalyze change on causes you care about.

Online Networks – Social media feeds, messaging platforms and discussion communities allowing networking across distances and potentially introducing you to contacts outside established networks through hashtags and viral posts.

The optimal network portfolio balances intimacy with diversity – containing both profoundly close tribal bonds (Dunbar suggested an upper cognitive limit of about 150 for stable social relationships) as well as wider "weak tie" access to fresh ideas and unforeseen possibilities. Different networks serve distinct needs while synergistically benefiting each other.

For example, a startup founder might convene a trusted personal advisory board for confidential counsel while also maximizing digital visibility and professional event networking to access investors. A healthy interplay enables advancing career objectives through aligning wider ecosystems while grounded by inner circles reminding greater purpose beyond profit and loss.

IV. How to Build Your Network

Expanding connections in an instrumental way while retaining authenticity requires thoughtfulness around conveying your innate value and understanding others' needs. Wider exposure remains pointless without showcasing your talents. Therefore:

- Identify what problems your passion, creativity and expertise might help solve for people in desired networks. What outcomes would contacts wish to achieve? Use this insight to design contributions of genuine worth.

- Start small within existing communities. Volunteer for speaking opportunities at a local meetup before chasing big stages. Offer neighbors helpful favors building localized goodwill. Master intimacy before breadth.

- Give more than you ask for, especially early on. Eager energy can repel, while modest acts of service attract. Follow founders like Facebook's Zuckerberg starting with university classmates before conquering global networks.

Importantly, avoid transactional networking relationships solely seeking personal gain. Demonstrate selfless caring first, asking thoughtful questions over speaking about yourself. The most powerful networks run not on quid pro quo bartering but rather shared meaning fueling generosity spreading ideas and opportunities organically.

V. The Art of Conversation in Networking

Skilled conversationalists breathe life into networks through uplifting interactions. Researchers have identified critical abilities underpinning connection including:

- Attentive Listening – Being fully present to understand contextual needs before seeking to be understood.

- Insightful Questioning - Curiosity exploring commonalities but also welcoming different worldviews.

- Vulnerability and Humor – Judicious sharing of real feelings and stories generating empathy while maintaining appropriate boundaries. Along with levity and playfulness!

These statutes elevate networking beyond exploitation by respecting fellow humans underlying all opportunities.

Of course, mastering networking as a high art rather than a transactional game presents a lifelong journey. Mentors provide integral guidance here through modeling dignified behaviors. Remember though that kind reception of your talents ultimately matters more than any scripted tactics. Focus first on developing creative skills the world genuinely requires, then pour that excellence freely into networks aligned with the causes and communities you care most about. The rest unfolds organically to those providing real value. Now venture forth and meaningfully engage!

VI. Digital Networking

While human connections ultimately drive impactful networking, social technologies exponentially expand access and efficiency. Platforms like LinkedIn and Twitter enable discovering contacts, sharing talents, directing serendipitous encounters and coordinating meetups.

Posting insights publicly builds authority and allows targeted outreach to high value contacts responsive to your messaging. For example, angel investor Jason Calacanis leveraged his popular blog and Twitter following to rapidly fund various startups.

Ensure your digital presence conveys professionalism and passion for helping others. Profiles should highlight skills, public talks, projects benefiting communities and recommendations. Develop content and connections over time rather than chasing viral randomness.

VII. Common Mistakes While Networking

When building networks, many well-intentioned attempts backfire. Avoid these common pitfalls:

- Focusing conversations excessively on yourself rather than learning about others' interests

- Collecting business cards without follow-up to strengthen bonds

- Neglecting personal networks assuming online contacts suffice

- Attending events without clear value-add to fellow attendees

- Leveraging contacts solely for selfish aims rather than mutual benefit

The antidote requires mindset adjustment from exploitation to service. Give first, listen deeply and enable community before requests.

VIII. Case Study – Successful Networkers

1. Keith Ferrazzi (born May 14, 1964 in Pennsylvania, USA)

Ferrazzi is an author and founder of research institute Ferrazzi Greenlight. He actively practices his relationship and networking principles outlined in his bestselling book "Never Eat Alone". For example, while working at Deloitte in the 1990s, Ferrazzi masterfully leveraged professional relationships and employed grassroots marketing to stand out in a competitive workplace and eventually become the company's youngest partner at the age of 34.

2. Naveen Jain (born September 6, 1959 in India)

Technology entrepreneur Jain co-founded information services company InfoSpace in 1996, which dominated the online services market in the late 90s. He credits networking skills for raising $80 million from high profile investors like Bill Gates and Paul Allen to rapidly grow InfoSpace. Jain carried those relationship building abilities to later found innovative companies like Moon Express and Viome.

3. Gwen Jimmere (born October 13, 1975 in Michigan, USA)

Jimmere is an activist, entrepreneur and founder of Naturalicious haircare products designed specifically for tight, curly textures. To spread awareness amidst challenges finding traditional retail and media exposure as a black female founder, Jimmere leveraged online communities and networking events to share her mission. Her perseverance won influential opportunities like an exhibition at the National Museum of African American History and Culture. She continues empowering women entrepreneurs of color.

Key Takeaways

1. Networking builds relationships enabling life's possibilities

2. Balance intimacy with diversity across network types

3. Convey value clearly and focus on mutual benefit

4. Social platforms expand reach but human bonds drive impact

5. Avoid common errors like self-focus or exploitation

IX. Conclusion

Networking well requires both science and art - strategic exposure combined with conversational intimacy, generosity and compassion. Start simply within existing communities. Share your talents while understanding colleague needs. Building trusting relationships rooted in mutual growth unlocks life's greatest rewards.

Exercises

- Audit your existing network types and contacts

- Craft a 25-word personal value statement

- Reach out to 3 peers to offer help without expectations

- Create social profiles conveying your talents/passions

- Attend local events to practice conversational skills

Chapter 14

Dating Smarts – Developing Healthy Romantic Relationships

I. Introduction

As a young adult, romantic relationships can feel exciting yet confusing. You may crave intimacy and connection but not know how to build fulfilling bonds. This chapter will equip you with 'dating smarts' - the knowledge and skills to develop healthy romantic relationships that enrich your life.

Why are dating smarts so crucial? Because romantic bonds profoundly impact well-being. Studies show relationships can buffer stress, provide meaning, and predict life satisfaction. But unhealthy bonds do the opposite, eroding self-worth, and mental health. By dating smart, you can cultivate relationships that help you flourish.

First, we will explore different relationship types and your needs within them. Next, we will outline key elements for healthy bonds like trust and communication. Then, we will turn to red flags that signal dysfunction. Armed with dating smarts, you can identify suitable partners, build robust relationships, and avoid unhealthy ones.

II. Understanding Relationships

Relationships exist on a spectrum, from casual to serious and long-term. To date smart, understand your needs and the type of bond you want.

Casual relationships offer intimacy without commitment. These can boost confidence and provide companionship. However, some struggle to avoid attachment in casual relationships, so reflect carefully on your needs.

Serious relationships involve commitment, sacrifice, and interdependence. This depth can foster tremendous personal growth. But serious bonds require vulnerability and trust in your partner. Not everyone desires this level of intimacy.

Long-term relationships like marriage involve the highest commitment. These relationships require tremendous work but can be deeply fulfilling. Before seeking this bond, ensure you and your partner share key values and life goals.

To date smart, reflect on your needs and the type of relationship you want before pursing bonds. As psychologist Ty Tashiro notes in The Science of Happily Ever After, relationships only succeed when grounded in self-knowledge. Understand your needs in a partner and type of bond before pursuing romance.

III. Building a Healthy Relationship

Once you enter a relationship, certain elements are vital for health. The first is open communication. As found by relationship researcher John Gottman, successful couples engage in frequent emotionally-attentive dialogue. Share your feelings, needs, hopes, fears, and quirks with your partner.

Next is trust. Couples therapist M. Gary Neuman finds trust is essential for relationship wellness. Let your partner in and provide emotional support. Be reliable and honest. Trust your partner unless given reason not to.

Respect is also vital. Never insult, shame, or manipulate your partner. Value their needs and listen nonjudgmentally. Research shows that respect predicts relationship satisfaction and longevity.

Additionally, maintain intimacy. Emotional and physical closeness strengthens bonds. Make time for affection and activities you both enjoy. Go on dates, cuddle, and express your love.

Finally, give your partner space to grow. Avoid excessive jealousy and control. As found by researcher Eli Finkel, allowing your partner autonomy paradoxically brings you closer.

Building these elements requires dedication. But healthy relationships profoundly enrich well-being. By dating smart and cultivating these factors, you can develop robust and fulfilling bonds.

IV. Red Flags in Relationships

While dating smart involves building healthy bonds, it also means spotting and avoiding dysfunction. Some key red flags indicating an unhealthy or potentially abusive relationship include:

Possessiveness - If your partner excessively tracks your time and location or isolates you from friends and family, this signals possessiveness, which often precipitates abuse. Listen to your discomfort.

Manipulation - Emotional manipulation like gaslighting or guilt-tripping should ring alarm bells. Healthy partners respect your emotions and needs.

Explosive Anger - Frequent intense outbursts of anger indicate poor self-regulation and emotional abuse. Non-abusive partners express anger calmly.

Disrespect - Partners who regularly insult, humiliate, or shame you do not respect you. This suggests they will not change.

Dishonesty - Relationships require truthfulness. Partners who compulsively lie breach trust in alarming ways.

These red flags often warn of escalating dysfunction. Ignoring them imperils well-being. Dating smart means recognizing unhealthy dynamics and leaving at the first signs of abuse. Rather than fix a partner, exit an unhealthy relationship and never look back. Your well-being must be the priority.

Sarah's Story

Sarah Les dated Daniel Ford for six months. Initially, he showered her with affection and compliments. But over time, his behavior changed. He demanded she account for where she was at all times. He would fly into a rage if dinner wasn't ready when he got home from work. One night, during an argument, Dan threw a plate against the wall inches from Sarah's head. Terrified, Sarah recognized his explosive anger was dangerous. She waited until Dan left for work the next morning, packed her belongings, and drove to her sister's home. Though heartbroken, Sarah knew she had to prioritize her safety. Dan's possessive, angry behaviors were clear red flags of abuse. By listening to her instincts and removing herself from the relationship, Sarah may have saved her own life.

Andrew's Story

Andrew West dated Elizabeth Smith for a year before she convinced him to let her move in. Soon, Liz began intercepting Andrew's mail and texts to "protect" him from exes. She falsely accused him of cheating regularly. One day, Liz smashed Andrew's laptop in a fit of jealous rage. Andrew recognized Liz's extreme possessiveness and explosive anger were unhealthy and dangerous. He broke up with Liz immediately and arranged for a police escort to ensure she vacated his apartment safely. Though the experience shook him, Andrew felt empowered trusting his judgment and enforcing his boundaries, even if it meant ending the relationship.

Jenna's Story

Jenna Spike and Mike Spaniard enjoyed a whirlwind romance and got engaged after four months. Soon after, Mike began insisting Jenna quit her job to plan their wedding. He picked fights over small issues and threatened to leave when he didn't get his way. One night, after Mike had too much to drink, he called Jenna worthless and pathetic. She recognized Mike's manipulative and disrespectful behavior were serious red flags. The next day, Jenna returned Mike's ring and broke off the engagement - one of the hardest things she'd ever done. But she knew she deserved better. Jenna's story reminds us that ending unhealthy relationships early on requires courage but protects our dignity and self-worth.

V. Breakups & Moving On

Ending relationships, even unhealthy ones, can be extremely difficult. When a bond you worked hard to build falls apart, the grief can feel overwhelming. However, breakups are often necessary for your health and happiness in the long-run. By handling them with grace and learning from the experience, you can emerge wiser and more empowered in relationships moving forward.

First, treat yourself and your partner compassionately during a breakup. Have an honest, gentle conversation and give one another space and time to process it. Reflect on what you learned, and do not place blame. Experts advise against "ghosting" or bitterly insulting exes, as these often reflect poorly on your character.

Next, remove physical reminders of the relationship from your living space. Put gifts and photos in storage temporarily to help you move forward. Lean on friends and family for support during this transitional time. Share your feelings to process them.

Further, rediscover activities and passions outside the relationship. Join new clubs, reconnect with friends, travel somewhere new. This will build confidence and remind you that you are a complete person, even without your ex.

Finally, reflect on any red flags you may have missed. Consider seeking counseling to unpack why you overlooked concerning behaviors. Use insights from the relationship to make better choices moving forward. With time and self-work, you can emerge wiser and empowered.

Key Takeaways

1. Understanding oneself is crucial before entering into any romantic relationship. Take time to identify your needs, values, and

relationship goals before pursuing bonds. Choose partners who complement and support your best self.

2. Communication, trust, and respect are vital for a healthy relationship. Develop emotional intimacy by sharing feelings openly and listening attentively. Build trust by being reliable, honest and respectful of boundaries. Validate your partner's emotions and needs.

3. It's important to recognize red flags early on in order to prevent potential harm or abuse. Devaluing comments, extreme jealousy, explosive anger, dishonesty, and possessiveness signal dysfunctional relationship dynamics. End concerning relationships early.

4. Breakups are part of life; they should be handled with grace and used as learning experiences. Display compassion, reflect on insights gained, rediscover your passions, and apply lessons to make better choices moving forward.

Exercises/Activities

Self-Reflection Questions:

- What are my top needs and values in a romantic partner and relationship? Be specific.

- What relationship expectations may I need to adjust to be realistic?

- What red flags and unhealthy behaviors would be deal-breakers for me?

Relationship Values Card Sort Activity:

- Cards with relationship values like honesty, intimacy, independence, laughter, calmness, spontaneity.

- Have reader sort cards from most to least important to them.

- Discuss how knowing your top values can guide partner selection and strengthen bonds.

Healthy Communication Techniques Worksheet:

- Provide examples of healthy communication techniques to practice like active listening, validating feelings, and taking breaks when agitated.

- Have reader write examples of applying these techniques to issues in their own relationships.

VI. Conclusion

Dating smarts enable you to flourish in romantic life. While relationships always require work, self-awareness helps you understand your needs, forge bonds with suitable partners, and recognize dysfunction early. Applying dating smarts leads to relationships that are emotionally enriching rather than depleting. You deserve to feel fulfilled, respected and heard in love. By setting standards and boundaries, communicating courageously, and continually growing, you can build a dating life that helps you feel safe, seen, and valued. You hold the pen; write your own beautiful love story.

Conclusion

Embracing Adulthood with Confidence and Resilience

Introduction

Throughout this book, we explored the key skills and mindsets required to successfully transition into adulthood. From managing finances to building healthy relationships, the chapters aimed to provide actionable advice to equip you for the opportunities and challenges of early adulthood.

Summary of Chapters

In Chapter 1, we discussed managing the emotional rollercoaster of your late teens and early twenties.

Chapter 2 focused on building self-confidence and discovering your authentic self. Chapter 3 covered developing independence and making informed decisions. Chapter 4 explored cultivating resilience and a growth mindset.

Additional chapters offered practical guidance on topics like job searching, budgeting, loans, communication, conflict resolution, and dating. Each chapter aimed to break down complex topics with actionable steps and exercises so you can effectively put the advice into practice.

Final Thoughts

As you conclude this book, remember that the journey to adulthood is a lifelong process of growth. Approach every new stage with openness, self-compassion, and a willingness to learn. You may stumble at times, but challenges are opportunities to expand your skills and wisdom.

Trust in your ability to continuously evolve. The foundations we built together in this book have prepared you to handle adulthood with maturity, insight and grace. Stay true to your values, embrace self-discovery, and your future will shine bright. Your story is yours to write - make it a remarkable one.

As the poet Rainer Maria Rilke wrote, "Let everything happen to you: beauty and terror. Just keep going. No feeling is final." There will be triumphs and tribulations as you embrace adulthood. But persist through all of it. Have faith in your ability to learn and grow. Be gentle with yourself in moments of fear, and keep your heart open to the insight gained during difficult times. If you maintain resilience and embrace each experience as part of your journey, you will flourish spectacularly.

I hope this book has provided a helpful guide as you navigate your transition to adulthood. You have so much to offer the world. Go forward with courage, stay humble and curious, and your light will illuminate the path for others. All the best on your journey ahead!

References

Books:

Adulthood in Emerging Adulthood: Transitions and Processes by Jeffrey Jensen Arnett (2015)

Aristotle. (c. 350 BCE). Nicomachean ethics (W.D. Ross, Trans.). Internet Classics Archive. (Original work published c. 350 BCE). https://classics.mit.edu/Aristotle/nicomachaen.html

Arnett, J. J. (2000). Emerging adulthood: A theory of development from the late teens through the twenties. American psychologist, 55(5), 469-480.

Arshad, M., Anderson, J., and Sharif, A. (2015). Comparison of Intuitionistic Fuzzy TOPSIS and Bayesian Belief Intuitionistic Fuzzy TOPSIS for Decision Making. International Journal of Innovative Computing, Information and Control, 11(5), 1681-1696.

Bandura, A. (1977). Self-efficacy: toward a unifying theory of behavioral change. Psychological review, 84(2), 191.

Beck, J. S. (2011). Cognitive behavior therapy: Basics and beyond. Guilford Press.

Bodie, S., Grainger, A., & Smith, G. (2015). Business communication for success: Essential skills for the modern business professional. Cengage Learning Australia.

De Dreu, C. K. W. (2008). The virtue and vice of workplace conflict: Food for (pessimistic) thought. Journal of Organizational Behavior, 29(1), 5-18.

Dweck, C. S. (2006). Mindset: The new psychology of success. Random House.

Ferrazzi, K. (2005). Never eat alone: And other secrets to success, one relationship at a time. Crown Business.

Finkel, E. J., & Campbell, W. K. (2001). Self-control and accommodation in close relationships: an interdependence analysis. Journal of personality and social psychology, 81(2), 263.

Finkel, E.J., Slotter, E.B., Luchies, L.B., Walton, G.M., & Gross, J.J. (2013). A brief intervention to promote conflict reappraisal preserves marital quality over time. Psychological Science, 24(8), 1595-1601.

Frei, J.R. and Shaver, P.R. (2002). Respect in close relationships: Prototype definition, self-report assessment, and initial correlates. Personal Relationships, 9(2), 121-139.

Gottman, J. M., & Silver, N. (2015). The seven principles for making marriage work. Harmony.

Häfner, A., Stock, A., & Oberst, V. (2015). Decreasing students' stress through time management training: an intervention study. European Journal of Psychology of Education, 30(1), 81-94.

Holt-Lunstad, J., Smith, T. B., & Layton, J. B. (2010). Social relationships and mortality risk: A meta-analytic review. PLoS Medicine, 7(7), e1000316.

Jain, N. (2017, June 5). If You Don't Network, You Won't Be Part of the AI Revolution. Entrepreneur.

Kohlberg, L. (1973). Continuities in childhood and adult moral development revisited. In P. B. Baltes & K. W. Schaie (Eds.), Life-span developmental psychology: Personality and socialization (pp. 179–204). Academic Press.

Kothari, R., Poudel, A., Khanal, P., Pandey, A., & Mathema, P. (2014). Interpersonal communication skills among undergraduate students at Patan Academy of Health Sciences: A student perspective. Journal of Patan Academy of Health Sciences, 1(1), 61-65.

Król, M. (2006). Vincent van Gogh and the contours of madness. Philosophy, Psychiatry, & Psychology, 13(4), 289-294.

Kurdek, L. A. (1994). Conflict resolution style and perception in adolescent romantic relationships. Developmental Psychology, 30(1), 109-115.

Laurenceau, J.-P., Barrett, L. F., & Pietromonaco, P. R. (1998). Intimacy as an interpersonal process: the importance of self-disclosure, partner disclosure, and perceived partner responsiveness in interpersonal exchanges. Journal of personality and social psychology, 74(5), 1238–1251.

McCrae, R. R., & Costa, P. T. (1989). Reinterpreting the Myers-Briggs Type Indicator from the perspective of the five-factor model of personality. Journal of personality, 57(1), 17-40.

Neuman, M. G. (2008). Emotional infidelity: How to afford your partner unlimited intimacy and still feel loved, respected and secure. HCI.

Orth, U., Robins, R. W., & Widaman, K. F. (2012). Life-span development of self-esteem and its effects on important life outcomes. Journal of personality and social psychology, 102(6), 1271.

Piaget, J. (1972). Intellectual evolution from adolescence to adulthood. Human Development, 15(1), 1-12.

Preston, S.D. and de Waal, F.B.M. (2002). Empathy: Its ultimate and proximate bases. Behavioral and Brain Sciences, 25(1), 1-20.

R.M. (1934). Letters to a Young Poet (S. Mitchell, Trans.). New York, NY: Norton. (Original work published 1929)

Rosenberg, M. (1965). Society and the adolescent self-image. Princeton, NJ: Princeton University Press.

Rotter, J. B. (1966). Generalized expectancies for internal versus external control of reinforcement. Psychological monographs: General and applied, 80(1), 1-28.

Rusbult, C. E., & Van Lange, P. A. M. (2003). Interdependence, interaction, and relationships. Annual Review of Psychology, 54, 351-375.

Ryan, R. M., & Deci, E. L. (2000). Self-determination theory and the facilitation of intrinsic motivation, social development, and well-being. American psychologist, 55(1), 68.

Seligman, M. E. (2006). Learned optimism: How to change your mind and your life. Vintage.

Steiger, A. E., Allemand, M., Robins, R. W., & Fend, H. A. (2014). Low and decreasing self-esteem during adolescence predict adult depression two decades later. Journal of personality and social psychology, 106(2), 325.

Steinberg, L., Icenogle, G., Shulman, E. P., Breiner, K., Chein, J., Bacchini, D., ... & Takash, H. M. (2018). Around the world, adolescence is a time of heightened sensation seeking and immature self-regulation. Developmental science, 21(2), e12532.

Tashiro, T. (2017). The science of happily ever after: What really matters in the quest for enduring love. Harlequin Nonfiction.

The Defining Decade: Why Your Twenties Matter and How to Make the Most of Them by Meg Jay (2011)

The Millionaire Next Door: The Surprising Secrets of America's Wealthiest People by Thomas J. Stanley & William D. Danko (2003) The Power of Habit: Why We Do What We Do in Life and Business by Charles Duhigg (2012)

Trueman, M., & Hartley, J. (1996). A comparison between the time-management skills and academic performance of mature and traditional-entry university students. Higher Education, 32(2), 199-215.

Trzesniewski, K. H., Donnellan, M. B., Moffitt, T. E., Robins, R. W., Poulton, R., & Caspi, A. (2006). Low self-esteem during adolescence predicts poor health, criminal behavior, and limited economic prospects during adulthood. Developmental psychology, 42(2), 381.

Walker, M. (2017, March 22). How This Entrepreneur Created an Internationally Recognized Brand with No Venture Capital. Black Enterprise.

Journals:

American Journal of Public Health: "Life Skills Education in High School: A Systematic Review" by Jessica T. Catalano & Amy R. Hawkins (2014)

Developmental Psychology: "The Development of Identity in Emerging Adulthood" by Jeffrey Arnett (2000)

Journal of Personality and Social Psychology: "Self-Esteem and Social Behavior" by Roy Baumeister & Robert F. Tice (1990)

Journal of Youth and Adolescence: "Resilience in Emerging Adulthood: A Review of Research and Implications for Practice" by Ann S. Masten (2004)

Psychological Science in the Public Interest: "Financial Literacy and Decision-Making" by Brad M. Klontz & Kathleen S. Bernhardt (2005)

Rath, T. (2006). StrengthsFinder 2.0. Gallup.

Nonviolent Communication: A Language of Life by Marshall B. Rosenberg (2013)

Websites:

General Resources:

National Institute of Mental Health: https://www.nimh.nih.gov/health/topics/child-and-adolescent-mental-health

The Jed Foundation: https://jedfoundation.org/

The Trevor Project: https://www.thetrevorproject.org/

American Psychological Association (APA) - Help Center: https://www.apa.org/

Chapter 1 - Transitioning from Teenage Years:

The Greater Good Science Center at the University of California, Berkeley: https://greatergood.berkeley.edu/

The Mayo Clinic - Coping with Teenage Stress: https://mcpress.mayoclinic.org/mental-health/tips-for-helping-children-deal-with-stress-2/

Chapter 2 - Navigating Identity:

Mind: https://www.mind.org.uk/

The National Center for Transgender Equality: https://transequality.org/

The Ruderman Foundation: https://rudermanfoundation.org/

Chapter 3 - Developing Independence:

Khan Academy: https://www.khanacademy.org/

Coursera: https://www.coursera.org/

The Balance Careers:
https://www.thebalancemoney.com/career-planning-6265513

Chapter 4 - Building Resilience and Growth Mindset:

Resilience: https://www.resilience.org/

Stanford University - Growth Mindset resources:
https://ctl.stanford.edu/growth-mindset

Chapter 5 - Job Search & Interview Skills:

Indeed: https://www.indeed.com/

LinkedIn: https://www.linkedin.com/

Glassdoor: https://www.glassdoor.com/index.htm

Chapter 6 & 7 - Personal Finance:

The National Endowment for Financial Education
(NEFE): https://www.nefe.org/

Investopedia: https://www.investopedia.com/

The Mint.com: https://mint.intuit.com/

Chapter 8 - Credit Score:

Annual Credit Report:
https://www.annualcreditreport.com/index.action

Consumer Financial Protection Bureau (CFPB):
https://www.consumerfinance.gov/

Chapter 9 - Student Loans & Scholarships:

Federal Student Aid: https://studentaid.gov/

Fastweb: https://www.fastweb.com/

The College Board: https://www.collegeboard.org/

Chapter 10 - Communication Skills:

Toastmasters International:
https://www.toastmasters.org/

Harvard Business Review:
https://hbr.org/2022/11/how-great-leaders-communicate

Chapter 11 & 12 - Interpersonal Skills & Conflict Resolution:

The Gottman Institute: https://www.gottman.com/

The National Conflict Resolution Center:
https://ncrconline.com/

Chapter 13 - Networking Skills:

Chamber of Commerce:
https://www.uschamber.com/

Meetup: https://www.meetup.com/

LinkedIn Alumni tool:
https://www.linkedin.com/learning/learning-linkedin-for-students-16915125/the-alumni-tool

Chapter 14 - Healthy Relationships:

The Gottman Institute (mentioned above)

Love is Respect: https://www.loveisrespect.org/

The National Domestic Violence Hotline:
https://www.thehotline.org/search-our-resources/

Printed in Great Britain
by Amazon

54800996R00145